# PRESIDENTS &
# THE PRESIDENCY

# PRESIDENTS &
# THE PRESIDENCY

Essays by

*Stephen Hess*

The Brookings Institution
*Washington, D.C.*

*Library of Congress Cataloging-in-Publication Data*

Hess, Stephen.
    Presidents & the Presidency / essays by Stephen Hess.
        p.   cm.
    Includes index.
    ISBN 0-8157-3632-0 (cloth)—ISBN 0-8157-3631-2 (pbk.)
    1. Presidents—United States.   I. Title.
    E176.1.H46   1995
    973′.099—dc20                                                    95-4429
                                                                        CIP

9 8 7 6 5 4 3 2 1

The paper used in this publication meets the minimum requirements
of the American National Standard for Information Sciences—
Permanence of Paper for Printed Library Materials,
ANSI Z39.48-1984.

Typeset in Bembo and Helvetica Condensed

Composition by AlphaTechnologies/mps, Inc.
Charlotte Hall, Maryland

Printed by R. R. Donnelley and Sons Co.
Harrisonburg, Virginia

# THE BROOKINGS INSTITUTION

The Brookings Institution is an independent organization devoted to nonpartisan research, education, and publication in economics, government, foreign policy, and the social sciences generally. Its principal purposes are to aid in the development of sound public policies and to promote public understanding of issues of national importance.

The Institution was founded on December 8, 1927, to merge the activities of the Institute for Government Research, founded in 1916, the Institute of Economics, founded in 1922, and the Robert Brookings Graduate School of Economics and Government, founded in 1924.

The Board of Trustees is responsible for the general administration of the Institution, while the immediate direction of the policies, program, and staff is vested in the President, assisted by an advisory committee of the officers and staff. The by-laws of the Institution state: "It is the function of the Trustees to make possible the conduct of scientific research, and publication, under the most favorable conditions, and to safeguard the independence of the research staff in the pursuit of their studies and in the publication of the results of such studies. It is not a part of their function to determine, control, or influence the conduct of particular investigations or the conclusions reached."

The President bears final responsibility for the decision to publish a manuscript as a Brookings book. In reaching his judgment on the competence, accuracy, and objectivity of each study, the President is advised by the director of the appropriate research program and weighs the views of a panel of expert outside readers who report to him in confidence on the quality of the work. Publication of a work signifies that it is deemed a competent treatment worthy of public consideration but does not imply endorsement of conclusions or recommendations.

The Institution maintains its position of neutrality on issues of public policy in order to safeguard the intellectual freedom of the staff. Hence interpretations or conclusions in Brookings publications should be understood to be solely those of the authors and should not be attributed to the Institution, to its trustees, officers, or other staff members, or to the organizations that support its research.

---

For Peter & Sara

# Foreword

As Stephen Hess starts his twenty-fifth year as a senior fellow at Brookings, we are pleased to publish two volumes of his essays about the institutions that have been the primary focus of his research here, *Presidents & the Presidency* and *News & Newsmaking*.

The American research organization, or think tank, of which Brookings is one of the oldest, has a role without precedent in other countries of serving as a way station for some people between periods of government service or between government service and a return to academia. This role encourages the interchange of ideas between those who practice and those who research public policy and produces solid analyses and recommendations based on experience and study.

The author's career illustrates one of these patterns. He came to Brookings after concluding two assignments for President Nixon, first as deputy assistant for urban affairs, serving in the White House as chief of staff to Daniel Patrick Moynihan, and then as the national chairman of the White House Conference on Children and Youth. Previously he had been a fellow at Harvard University's Institute of Politics and a speechwriter for President Eisenhower.

While at Brookings Mr. Hess has engaged in both research and policy application. He has served as U.S. delegate to the UN General

Assembly in New York, U.S. delegate to the UNESCO General
Conference in Paris, editor in chief of a national Republican platform, and adviser to the Carter administration on the structuring of
the Executive Office of the President. He has also served on the
Washington, D.C., board of higher education, which created the
University of the District of Columbia during his tenure, and as
chairman of a commission that assisted in reordering government
from an appointed to an elected city council.

Brookings scholars are encouraged to test their ideas in the class-
room as well as in government service. Mr. Hess has taught courses
on the interaction between government and the media at the John
F. Kennedy School at Harvard University and at Johns Hopkins
University. At the University of Southern California in Los Angeles
he created a course on the presidency using tapes of interviews he
had conducted with presidential assistants who dated back to Franklin Roosevelt's administration.

The essays in this volume are collected to give the reader a
window into the author's approach to research and problem solving
and a feel for the Washington that has been his venue during a
challenging and sometimes dramatic era. Their publication has been
supported by a grant from the Cissy Patterson Trust.

The manuscript benefited from the critiques of Thomas E. Mann
and Bruce K. MacLaury; the administrative support of Cynthia
Terrels, Inge Lockwood, and Susan A. Stewart; and the research
assistance of Fawn Johnson. The pages were proofread by Ellen
Garshick, and Julia Petrakis compiled the index. The book was
edited by James R. Schneider, who has worked with Mr. Hess for
more than a decade.

The views expressed in these essays are those of the author and
should not be ascribed to the trustees, officers, or other staff members
of the Brookings Institution.

*December 1995*                                   Michael H. Armacost
*Washington, D.C.*                                         *President*

# Contents

# Author's Note

The essays in this volume have been revised since their initial publication, but no consistent or wide-ranging attempt has been made to update the observations. In addition, in the interests of readability for wider audiences, the scholarly footnotes that accompanied most of the essays at their first publication have been dropped. Those readers who are interested in checking sources should consult the version of the essay cited at the bottom of each opening page.

# Introduction:
# My Presidency

Each of us has a personal presidency relating to our own experiences and a generational presidency that we share with others of our age, a *my* presidency and an *our* presidency. For me, born a month after Franklin D. Roosevelt was inaugurated, my first memory of there being a president was during the 1940 election campaign when I was in second grade and got into a fierce fight with Herb Kaufman over who was best, Roosevelt or Willkie. We did not have the foggiest idea of what we were fighting about, of course, yet this was the beginning of our generational presidency. My personal presidency began four years later when I waved to President Roosevelt as he drove down Broadway in an open car in a cold rain. (Had I been a scholar or a journalist I might have known the political importance of what I was witnessing. Roosevelt's four-hour rain-soaked drive was designed to dispel rumors of his ill health.)

How forming is our generational presidency? How much of our concept of the office is apt to have been shaped by these early impressions? Studies of political socialization demonstrate that I was a pretty typical kid in that most of us have our first recognition of government in the person of the president when we are in second or third grade. By late high school we have a more serious impression of presidents. So to the degree that I was locked into a presidency, it

1

was the heroic presidency of FDR, a leader who successfully brought us through the Great Depression and a just war against Germany and Japan.

But what of my eldest son, born in 1961, whose first presidential recognition was of Lyndon Johnson and Washington burning (1968) and whose first presidential impression was of Jimmy Carter and long gas lines (1977)? Is he equally possessed of an idealized presidency? And what will be my granddaughter's, who will recognize a president in 2002?

The scholarly answer is we do not know. That part of political science that deals with this subject had been a robust field in the 1950s and 1960s. (Indeed, it was so robust that scholars were already fighting methodological battles.) And then just as suddenly it dropped off the academic radar screen. In one of the last great studies, *Children in the Political System* (1969), David Easton and Jack Dennis, after interviewing more than 12,000 children, concluded, "We were unable to find a child who did not express the highest esteem for the President." But there are only clues as to the attitudes of these children in later years and of subsequent American children. In the Watergate year of 1973, Fred I. Greenstein (in his best Art Linkletter manner) asked children to finish this story: "One day the President was driving his car to a meeting. Because he was late, he was driving very fast. The police stop the car. . . ." To complete the tale, 20 percent of these Nixon-era children told Greenstein that their generational presidency was "angry, annoyed, unfriendly, arrogant; unfairly sacks policeman, threatens to sack policeman, speeds off again after being stopped, drives off in a huff, refuses to pay the fine, argues with the policeman, pulls rank arrogantly." A larger 1973 study by F. Christopher Arterton of Boston third-, fourth- and fifth-graders contended "the effect of Watergate has been to transform the president into the malevolent leader."

Political scientists (along with psychologists) place great emphasis on early experiences: "what is learned first is learned best," and so forth. When it comes to presidents, I was reminded of this from a "Home Forum" essay in the *Christian Science Monitor* (February 28, 1995) by Richard Alder:

I must have been three or four years old the first time I saw that Norman Rockwell picture of Dwight D. Eisenhower. It must have been then, because my brother was a babe in arms, and I was becoming fast friends with Mark Rode, who lived up the street.

The picture was taped up in his mother's kitchen above the counter to the right of the doorway leading to the stairs.

I once asked Mark's mother who the man in the picture was.

"That's the president of the United States, President Eisenhower," she said.

"Why do you have a picture of the president here?" I asked, pointing to it.

"Because when I look at him and see his smile, I know everything is all right."

Mark's mother obviously shares with me a sunny presidency, which we could no more shed than Richard Alder is able to forget Ike's smile. Nor will our presidencies fail to reflect the add-on experiences of living through the Kennedy-Johnson-Nixon-Ford-Carter-Reagan-Bush-Clinton years. It is not very different from the experiences of Lord Bryce, who visited America during the presidencies of Ulysses S. Grant, Rutherford B. Hayes, and Chester A. Arthur, and then wrote his famous 1888 treatise, "Why Great Men Are Not Elected Presidents." But Mark's mother and I are the lucky ones. Some of our generation turned against our presidency, disillusioned, in much the manner of a Whittaker Chambers rejecting the communism of his youth.

I continue to retain an optimistic view of the office and its potential, if not always its practitioners. (A large part of this optimism is more probably attributable to my genes than to my experience.) One characteristic of this optimism has been the accent on fine-tuning, what Charles Krauthammer calls "the structural fix." Since the institution of the presidency is essentially sound, I argue, all that is needed are changes around the margins. Rereading these thoughts on the presidency reminds me of my shady past exploring such proposals as a national primary (no) or a six-year, one-term presidency (no) or repealing the Twenty-second Amendment (yes) or a new way to choose vice presidential candidates (yes) or even my personal favorite, moving elections to the last day in May with the inauguration on July 4. (At the same time always worrying about the unanticipated consequences.)

Another theme to which I keep returning is the need to strengthen political parties—a fertile area for fine-tuning—and the extent to which I blame problems of the presidency on the decline of parties. This is also a constant refrain of my friend David S. Broder, the columnist, both of us being products of undergraduate education at a time (the 1950s) when political science departments were debating the recommendations of a report titled *Toward a More Responsible Two-Party System*.

If children are, in a sense, born into a presidency, they are also taught into a presidency. Paul Samuelson, who wrote the very successful college economics textbook, has said, "I don't care who writes a nation's laws—or crafts its advanced treaties—if I can write its economic textbooks." Without making similar claims for courses in American government, Thomas Cronin in 1970 examined the presidency as it was portrayed in 1955–70 college-level textbooks, and found "the textbook presidency describes and extols a chief executive who is generally benevolent, omnipotent, omniscient, and highly moral. . . . What resulted very much was a storybook view that whatever was good for our president must be the right thing."

A decade later, after Vietnam and Watergate, Douglas Hoekstra reported on the textbooks of 1974–80: those of the "orthodoxy," he noted, now accented checking presidential power, stressing the useful constraints on what a president can do, while a new group of radical textbooks described presidents as playing "an active role [in] indoctrinating the American people into the ideology of the politico-economic establishment."

Today's textbooks, I discovered after a much more casual perusal than Cronin and Hoekstra, are no longer heavily ideological. Indeed, they have become intellectually bland (even when written by some notably unbland scholars). I suspect that what has happened is that textbook publishing has become so competitive and so potentially lucrative that the books' tone is largely influenced by market forces. Books are revised frequently, presumably to force students to buy a new edition instead of the used copy of a friend who took the course last year. Presumably the latest, version becomes a selling point when wooing professors who are bombarded with options.

Inherent in the new-style textbook, however, is a distortion that comes from being the latest, most up-to-date. The 1992–94 books that I examined devote an excessive amount of space to the present president. This tends to create an optical illusion that what is closest to the camera's lens is not only biggest but also most important. Here is the opening of the presidency chapter in a popular textbook by Theodore J. Lowi and Benjamin Ginsberg: "George Bush spent eight years in the vice-presidency as a 'yes man' to President Reagan. . . . Yet, as soon as he was inaugurated in January 1989, President Bush became a strong chief executive." The first six words of the presidency chapter by Kenneth Janda, Jeffrey M. Berry, and Jerry Goldman are "Read my lips: No new taxes." Professors preferring to assign another leading textbook by Everett Carll Ladd were told in December 1992, a month after the election, that by March they would have a chapter offering "a first look at the direction the new Clinton administration is taking in policy." A corollary to the adage "the Supreme Court follows the election returns" might be "so too do American government textbooks."

If 1950s textbooks erred by overgeneralizing, creating an immutable and unchanging presidential portrait (based on the twelve-plus Roosevelt years of the authors' generational presidency), the current textbook writers need to worry about producing a singularly solipsistic view of presidents in which what you see is all there is. Still, today's errors are less egregious.

Textbooks are also very much more attractive, filled with photographs, cartoons, graphs, and minidebates, whereas all I can remember of my days as a student are page after page of long gray paragraphs. There is no need to be stuffy about trying to appeal to readers who have been weaned on MTV. Yet neither should we confuse the clutter of factoids and sidebars in the new-style textbook with providing historical perspective or promoting a systematic understanding of the processes of government.

The media's role is modest in this process of creating our presidency, I believe, a paradox perhaps in a society where we learn about presidents primarily from television. But television is a for-profit division of the entertainment industry, catering to the consumers of a uniquely apolitical nation. Government is far down the list of subjects we wish to be entertained by. Moreover, the professionally sanctioned norms of "objective" news reporting, first invented by the wire services, also happen to be good for business. Mainstream American journalism believes in producing information that is the least offensive to the most people. This does not mean that reporting is without bias; since the skewing is against incumbents, the presidency always loses. Still, the media's political influence comes late—youngsters are not big news consumers, and those who become the big consumers are the most politically engaged, and so the least impressionable. The press is very important to presidents, of course, but largely around the edges where legislative agendas are fought and elections are won or lost.

My personal presidency has been fortunate enough to include service on two White House staffs and some odd jobs for two other presidents. In studying the presidency the trick is to sort out which characteristics are special to the occupant of the office and which transcend the individual.

When I first worked at the White House, it was at the end of an administration; the next time was at a beginning. From these experiences it was clear that certain things about the presidency have to do with endings and beginnings. A president is pushed along by the presidency's timeline. We are most attentive to time and the presidency when the issue is how fast a new chief executive should come out of the starting blocks, the so-called one hundred days. But there is just as much of a temporal reality to year four or year eight.

At the same time I learned that how presidents organize the White House staff, a matter of considerable interest to the White House press corps and increasingly to scholars, has more to do with presidents than with the presidency. While I was at the Eisenhower White House there was a major personnel change—the forced resignation of Chief of Staff Sherman Adams—which was expected to have consequences for the presidency. Yet the presidency did not change, just as it did not change when Richard Nixon replaced Bob Haldeman with Alexander Haig. Eisenhower, a president who understood organization, once said, "Organization cannot make a genius out of an incompetent. On the other hand, disorganization can scarcely fail to result in inefficiency." He knew that this was not a defining characteristic of the presidency.

These essays were written over a period of fifteen years. The chief criterion for inclusion here is survivability: Do they still say something useful about the presidency or a specific president? Take the case of "Presidential Qualities," the subject of the first essay, originally published in 1974 when Nixon was president and twice revised. The question it addresses is what characteristics should we want in a chief executive regardless of whether we agree with him or not? "Why Great Men Are Not Chosen Presidents: Lord Bryce Revisited" asks whether changes in the process by which we select presidential candidates would result in different kinds of persons seeking the presidency. "Toward a More Functional Presidency," written after Watergate, rethinks the appropriate role of the president and offers a job description. Because of my personal presidency, I have also taken the liberty of including "Nixon in Exile, 1961–1968," reflections on a relationship with the man who would soon become president.

The shape of the presidency in political science scholarship is neatly mirrored in American government textbooks. The durable persuasiveness of Richard E. Neustadt's *Presidential Power: The Politics of Leadership*, first published in 1960, has been passed along to students for a generation. For awhile in the 1970s James David Barber's emphasis on presidential personality was an integral part of presidency chapters. If there is to be a new pacesetter, let it be *The Presidency in a Separated System* (1994) by Charles O. Jones. Jones's thesis is that the presidency exists and must function within a system of separated institutions competing for power. This useful corrective to the presidency-centered model of American government became especially timely after Newt Gingrich became Speaker of the House in 1995. Given our marvelously complex system, how does one understand, explain, and teach 1995–96 Washington? President vs. Congress? Democrats vs. Republicans? Liberals vs. Conservatives? House vs. Senate? House Republicans vs. Senate Republicans? The answer, of course, is all of the above. And this is before one adds bureaucracy, advocacy groups, media, and governments at other levels.

It would be refreshing to see the academy awake to a Jonesian (or Madisonian) vision. But complexity conspires against this happen-

ing. As Jones himself pointed out in his 1994 address as president of
the American Political Science Association, undergraduate courses,
graduate study, faculty hiring, research, learned journals—all encourage division or specialization. So like any contact sport, we
shake hands, and then take the field as presidentialists or con-
gressionalists. The same is true of journalism in Washington, where
reporters are assigned to the White House beat or the Capitol Hill
beat and are not expected to move with their stories from one
location to the other.

Moreover, the presidency is too intoxicating, a president too
susceptible to heroic imagery, the White House too convenient a
location at which to park our hopes. Be warned of some of these
sentiments in the following pages. (As I've worked at pointing out,
that is from whence I come!) Still, we wear a truth-in-poli-sci label:
everything relates to everything else.

# Presidential
# Qualities

Max Frankel, the executive editor of the *New York Times* in 1987, told his staff that American presidents "have no 'right' of privacy. Their lives, their personalities, their finances, their families, friends and values are all fair game for fair reporting." Being able to be a public person is clearly a presidential quality. This means more than being capable of holding public office and assuming public responsibilities. Presidents must be willing to be exposed, to become public property, different only in degree from the White House in which they sleep and work and may have to raise their children. The people have the right of inspection, and those places that are put off limits are automatically suspect. The exposure of the president may be akin to a perpetual house and garden tour, with a steady stream of strangers passing through, fingering the furniture as well as the presidential ego. As television reporter Sam Donaldson told President Carter, "We're going to cover you one way or the other."

The loss of privacy is nearly total. Presidents' pasts are a matter of open discussion. When they are ill, their bodily functions are the subject of news briefings. Their friends become celebrities by definition, their families monuments on which the public can scrawl

From *The Presidential Campaign*, 3d ed. (Brookings, 1988).

graffiti, even their pets the First Dog or Cat. This extension of the presidency to include the president's private life is a twentieth-century phenomenon; there is nothing comparable in the earlier history of the country. It is a by-product of breakthroughs in communications technology: as the means and capacity to distribute information increased, making the information business highly profitable, presidents, their families, and their friends became the raw material that fueled a major industry. The trend is irreversible.

The loss of privacy necessarily becomes intimately bound up with the conduct of the office. Any description of the political techniques employed by presidents would differ little from those used by corporate executives, union leaders, or academic administrators. All these leaders offer rewards or withhold rewards with varying degrees of subtlety; all assess the strengths and weaknesses of supporters and opponents; all seek ways to build constituencies and to minimize opposition. What differs is the public aspect of presidential politics. The politics of business, union, and university are essentially private—played out within the confines of boardroom, union hall, and faculty commons. The U.S. Senate provides a public platform for its members, but Senate politics, conducted in cloakroom and conference committee, also are relatively private. Only presidents must have the ability to conduct their business without a hiding place.

Thus the presidential quality of being a public person, which assumes a willingness to abandon the sense of privacy, becomes essential to the operation of democratic government. Even though "the loss of respect for privacy has exacted a terrible price in American politics," as Anthony Lewis has written, no open society can afford a private presidency. The openness of the presidential office is the best insurance that there will be no dark corners where Watergate-type corruption can breed and that public policy will be properly ventilated before being approved.

Theodore E. Sorensen, President Kennedy's top White House aide, has stated that a president "must be at home with a staggering range of information. . . . He must know all about the ratio of cotton acreage to prices, of inventory accumulations to employment, of corporate investment to earnings, of selected steel prices to the economy, and of the biological effects of fallout to the effects of natural radiation." This image of the presidency as requiring an intellectual Hercules is unfair to the person in the White House and to the electorate. It is untrue that presidents need know "all about" an almost infinite range of recondite matters, any more than university chancellors need know all about macroeconomics, clinical psychology, microbiology, and linguistics to run their institutions. What presidents need know is whose advice to seek: can one person give full and dispassionate information or should competing experts be consulted? Which subjects are important now, and which may be important in the near future? When must decisions be made? What might be the consequences if no decision is made or if someone else is allowed to make a decision? These, rather than the ratio of cotton acreage to prices, are the sorts of things presidents need know.

Yet Sorensen is correct if he means that a president's intelligence must be broadly based. Above all, presidents should have wide interests and concerns. The problems of the country are diverse and interrelated. Presidents must indeed respond to particular crises as they arise and often must compartmentalize their attention to conform with governmental timetables—there is a time to prepare a budget, a time to deliver the economic report to the Congress, and so forth. But it is only the ability to keep many balls in the air that can harmonize national needs and aspirations. Bill Moyers, who was President Johnson's press secretary, recalls the White House during the winter of 1965 when the crucial decisions were made to escalate the war in Vietnam: "The President was—we were all—caught up in presenting the Great Society legislation to Congress. . . . Vietnam seemed to be more of a nuisance than a menace." Similarly, Richard Tanner Johnson wrote in *Managing the White House* that President Kennedy viewed Berlin as his big problem and perhaps did not have enough residual energy to consider carefully the consequences of U.S. involvement in Vietnam.

The electorate has a right to expect certain executive talents in all presidents. Many students of the presidency, however, have downgraded these skills. James MacGregor Burns has gone so far as to completely separate leadership from management. Leaders, he has stated, should be concerned with "goals rather than methods"; executive qualities are "secondary matters." None of the seven qualities singled out by presidential scholar Clinton Rossiter is executive. But presidents preside at the top of a vast enterprise. Their primary executive skills will be in choosing personnel and arriving at decisions. Some people can make up their minds about complex matters faster than others. Some have instincts—and the luck—that enable them to pick the right people for the right jobs, to find advisers who compensate for their own weaknesses, to get people to work together for a common cause, and to know when to discipline their subordinates.

Presidents must choose the decisions they wish to make. They cannot possibly make all decisions in an undertaking that employs millions of people. They must not be "nibbled to death by the guppies of minor or marginal issues," as presidential adviser Bryce Harlow once put it. Nor can presidents allow themselves to be overtaken by events and swept along by the actions of subordinates. They should populate the White House with advisers capable of sorting out problems for presidential attention. They should appoint department and agency heads who can manage their operations effectively and represent the president faithfully to Congress, the bureaucracy, and their constituents. Presidents must resist the temptation of allowing the White House to become "operational"—as the Tower commission's investigation of the Iran-contra affair explained after the fact to Ronald Reagan in 1987.

At the same time, presidents must resist being captured by the departments' perceptions of reality. They must arrive at decisions and make them known in ways that do not undermine those who must carry them out. Presidents must also prod appointees and civil servants to provide better information, more efficient operations, and more humane services. All of this must be done without the tools most executives in the private sector have. Government responds more to persuasion than to hierarchal command, its funding is not under executive control, and its employees are largely outside the president's power to hire and fire.

One presidential quality that perhaps we can take for granted is stamina. Presidents are elected to lead the government, and we expect them to have the energy to match the task. Some observers, however, contend that no president ever died of overwork. In *The Twilight of the Presidency*, George E. Reedy graphically showed that a president's days are as painless as staff, technology, and creature comforts allow. Historically the point is well taken: James K. Polk came closest to working himself to death, and even he survived his presidential term. Indeed, historian Thomas A. Bailey computed in 1966 that when assassinations are factored out, presidents have lived beyond their actuarial life expectancy.

Depending on the problems that urgently call for attention in their administrations, presidents may benefit from the expertise they bring to the office. Dwight Eisenhower's military background was uniquely suited to making cuts in the defense budget after the Korean War. Especially in conducting foreign policy—given the speed of events, the potential gravity of acting or not acting, and the secrecy often required—chief executives will be particularly advantaged by specialized knowledge. Richard Nixon's extensive travels in Asia led to reopening relations with the People's Republic of China. Lyndon Johnson, however, had little experience with or interest in foreign affairs when he came to office. In his handling of the Vietnam War, the problem was not that the president received one type of advice exclusively. The Defense Department pressed for increased involvement and the Central Intelligence Agency reported that the war was not going well. Perhaps U.S. commitments in Vietnam might have been of a different order if Johnson had had a background more suited to weighing the competing advice he was given.

High intelligence should not be confused with intellectuality, which need not be a presidential quality. Indeed, an intellectual may be at some disadvantage in the White House. Woodrow Wilson, the former professor who envisioned the League of Nations as the foundation of world peace, refused to make the concessions necessary to get the League treaty through the U.S. Senate. The intellectual may have difficulty translating thoughts into the common idiom, or may be removed by class and background and experience from the immediate concerns that presidents are expected to deal with, or may be incapable of taking prompt action because of a disinclination to base decisions on imperfect information or reduce complexities to terms that can be dealt with in the political process. Harry Truman wrote of his decision to use the atomic bomb, "Let there be no mistake about it. I regarded the bomb as a military weapon and never had any doubt that it should be used." Truman won the praise of European statesman Jean Monnet for having "the ability to decide." The best definition of the democratic statesman remains Walter Bagehot's "an uncommon man of common opinions."

Presidents must have a transcending honesty. After a period of corruption, integrity may be sufficient reason to elect a person, and the act of being honest may be deemed an important public service, as it was in the presidencies of Calvin Coolidge and Gerald Ford, which followed the major scandals of Teapot Dome and Watergate. But the electorate does not confuse honesty with ability. The same principle applies to courage. Presidents must have the courage to swim against the tide, the courage to take unpopular actions, and the courage not to act, which sometimes can be the greatest courage of all. John Adams had the courage not to go to war with France, for example, after the XYZ Affair, which appeared to be a French demand for a bribe from the U.S. government. But presidents can also make courageously bad decisions. Some have put Kennedy's decision to invade Cuba at the Bay of Pigs in this category.

What presidents need even more than honesty or courage, however, is the type of sensitivity that "Uncle Joe" Cannon, a Speaker of the U.S. House of Representatives, believed came from having one's ears full of grasshoppers because they were so close to the ground. Presidents must have a feel of the nation—understand the people's hopes and fears—and have a strong sense of the concrete. They must understand that they preside over a nation of individuals and that their policies affect people individually.

Yet almost everything that happens after a new president steps inside the White House makes it difficult to consider the effects on individuals. Information is collectivized: the goods that workers produce and the services they perform become the gross national product; people become the raw data for tabulations, percentages, and trends. What presidents know of the American people they must learn before they reach the presidency. Once surrounded by the Secret Service and the Signal Corps and reporters, they will continue to be seen by the people and occasionally even be touched by the people, but they will learn about them primarily through the media, public opinion polls, and their advisers inside and outside government. They will stop learning directly from the people.

Political intuition tells presidents whether they must inch toward a goal or can strike boldly, how flexible they need be, and how best to deploy their powers to gain the support they need. There is a sharp edge to the political qualities that we expect in our presidents. We expect them to maneuver, compromise, arm-twist, threaten—all in our best interests. These are standards of behavior that differ markedly from those we value in our personal relations. They are difficult to bring into harmony with ethical teachings. Of all twentieth-century presidents, the two Roosevelts came closest to having the kinds of political qualities that allowed them to perform their duties most effectively. Both were seekers of power with a single-minded intensity, experts at manipulation, with the ability to reverse field quickly. We might have desired them to be people of inestimable goodness, as was William Howard Taft. But it was advantageous to the nation that the Roosevelts were master politicians, whereas Taft's personal goodness proved only modestly useful in the absence of political skills.

The Roosevelts also were strongly exhibitionistic. Not all presidents have to have their well-developed dramatic instincts and their appreciation of the mysteries of making news. But all presidents must find ways to communicate, to persuade the people, and to arouse and enlist support. Ronald Reagan was derisively called "The Great Communicator" by his detractors, but the appellation reflected the fact that he possessed a unique presidential quality.

The ability to use the White House to create consensus, ease fears, and restore confidence—that is, to communicate—assumes a style that is acceptable to a majority of the people. Past presidential styles have varied from the laconic leadership of Coolidge to the calm grandfatherliness of Eisenhower to the boyish exuberance of Kennedy. But at a minimum, presidential style assumes a background without serious blemishes or, since there is a sort of statute of limitations in politics, only blemishes of ancient vintage that have been expiated or excused by the electorate. Every year some library committee takes offense at books by a James Joyce or a Henry Miller, but despite the Mrs. Grundy image of America as a nation of official puritans, Americans have consistently shown a sophisticated view of sexual conduct as a potential disqualification for the presidency. Comments and speculation on intimate relationships have sometimes figured in presidential campaigns: Jefferson and a black slave; Jackson's wife, who was a bigamist; Cleveland's illegitimate child;

Clinton's appearing on *60 Minutes* to dispute accusations that he had
had extramarital affairs. Still, never has that aspect been a determining factor. Even Gary Hart's decision to leave the Democratic
presidential race in 1987 had more to do with his exercising bad
judgment than with his offending the electorate's sense of acceptable
sexual behavior.

Shady financial dealings have been far more decisive, as was best
illustrated in the contest of 1884, when Grover Cleveland, who was
accused of fathering an illegitimate child, ran against James C. Blaine,
who was accused of receiving a veiled bribe from an Arkansas
railroad. In that election, a Chicago man wrote to a newspaper, "I
gather that Mr. Cleveland has shown high character and great
capacity in public office but that in private life his conduct has been
open to question, while on the other hand, Mr. Blaine in public life
has been weak and dishonest while he seems to have been an
admirable husband and father. The conclusion that I draw from these
facts is that we should elect Mr. Cleveland to the public office which
he is so admirably qualified to fill and remand Mr. Blaine to private
life which he is so eminently fitted to adorn." The voters agreed.

Presidents may lose their tempers, as Truman did when his
daughter Margaret's singing received a bad review, and they may
wear loud sport shirts. Such actions might even increase their popular standing unless they are seen as compromising effective presidential decorum. And Americans do not automatically equate decorum
with solemnity or middle-class behavior. While we are basically a
middle-class country, we have elected and taken pride in a collection of
patrician presidents. Presidents need not be like us, and it may help if
they are not, if only because we think it less likely that the rich will steal
from the public till. Some show of wealth does not offend most of us,
perhaps because most of us would like to be wealthy or because we may
think that wealth reflects special talents of those who have made it or
signals good omens for those who have been born with it—especially
since by seeking elective office the rich are asking to serve us, asking to
be commoners. When Pierre S. du Pont IV, a former governor of
Delaware, announced that he was seeking the 1988 Republican presidential nomination, E. J. Dionne reported in the *New York Times* that
he "bears one of the most illustrious names in American business" and
that he "prefers to be known as Pete."

A more subtle presidential quality is a sense of history. Not, as Joseph Kallenbach wrote, a reliance on history "to make the most of precedents established by his predecessors, and to see in the problems confronting him replicas of problems confronting chief executives in the past," for precedents are always available to buttress a position, and history repeats itself only in the most general terms. Rather, presidents need a sense of history that provides the understanding of what must be preserved and protected in the country, such as individual freedom, human dignity, and political democracy. It is an understanding of history that locates for presidents where they fit into the constitutional scheme of things, keeping them in phase with the other forces in government so that they are neither steamroller nor pushover in their relations with the Congress, courts, and states. In this sense a president's understanding of history becomes a restraint on despotism.

This historical sense should also provide the perspective to resist fads and passions of the moment. Unfortunately, the "exalting thought that he sits in Lincoln's seat" (as Clinton Rossiter put it) is capable of producing a touch of megalomania in a president. American history, with its play of fortuity, should be more humbling.

The ultimate usefulness of a president's personal qualities is to inspire public trust. This is not the same as being loved or noncontroversial. Nor can it be defined solely by style or personality, although style and personality can help inspire trust; nor by programs or ideologies, although these too help. It does not mean trust by everyone but trust by enough citizens to ensure that the social fabric will remain intact and that some effective action can be taken. Some equate trust with lack of pomp and recommend establishing it by abolishing the twenty-one-gun salutes, the honor guards, the red carpets, the elaborate state dinners, the presidential hideaways. This was the logic behind many of the symbolic acts taken by President Carter early in his administration, such as his limiting the number of White House limousines and the playing of "Hail to the Chief." However, Herbert Hoover's loss of trust was hardly due to excessive pomp, and the disposing of presidential yachts by Kennedy and Nixon did not measurably affect the people's trust in them one way or another.

The elements that go into inspiring trust are a style that is not offensive to the majority, a transcending honesty, a high level of intelligence, a willingness to deal with problems that immediately touch people's lives, a sense of patriotism, and public confidence in those to whom presidents lend their prestige and authority. What we expect in presidents we also expect in those around them, though to a lesser degree. This encompasses their families and associates in descending order of importance down to members of their political parties.

Finally, to aspire to more than adequacy, presidents must dream grandly, have goals and direction, and, if possible, offer concrete proposals when they take office. Yet this is not necessary for every president; there are moments that call for marking time, for consolidation. One problem with many theories of the presidency is the assumption that all presidents must be heroic and must interpret their powers with what Louis Koenig has called "maximum liberality." But all presidents should desire to leave the nation better than they find it, be able to push to some extent against the limits of what is considered feasible, and exhibit a generosity of spirit that seeks to bring out what is best in the people.

# Ike after
# Twenty-Five
# Years

The cheering had long ago stopped and now the old soldiers were returning to the scene of past political battles. It was 1978, twenty-five years after the presidential inauguration of Dwight D. Eisenhower, and the survivors of his White House staff—me included—were holding a reunion in Washington. We reminisced about the good old days, and while they were never quite as good as we now remember them, Eisenhower's way of running the White House still holds lessons for anyone concerned about the effectiveness of the presidency.

The command of armies had given Eisenhower a strong sense of the need to delegate responsibilities in large enterprises. He was impatient of those who brought him matters that he felt were not of presidential importance and should have been decided at lower levels. Some might contend that he left too many decisions to others. But from the perspective of a quarter century, it would be hard to point to a major action of his administration that he had not personally approved. Moreover, his habits of delegation encouraged his assistants to grow in competence and created a level of morale among political executives that has not been surpassed by other modern presidents.

*Baltimore Sun*, February 20, 1978, and other papers.

We have been told, in contrast, that Jimmy Carter's style is to draw into the Oval Office decisions of the most modest significance, including who can play tennis on the White House court. If this has not yet created bottlenecks, it is only because of Carter's remarkable energy, which, over time, must wear down. The depressing effect on staff morale, if not now apparent, is certainly predictable.

Eisenhower had a more structured staff system than Carter. Papers went to and from the president in an orderly fashion; reports were made on time; memos were routed to all those whose opinions were needed. It may be that highly creative people feel constrained by structure. But it is also true that at the Eisenhower White House no important papers got lost in transit.

On important matters, Eisenhower liked to get his information from listening; Carter, it is said, likes to get his from reading. A small point, perhaps. Yet advisers are inclined to say things to presidents that they may be unwilling to commit to paper, especially since presidential archives are eventually opened to the public. As a rule, the reading president makes more efficient use of his time; the listening president gets more subtle and variegated advice.

The White House staff under Eisenhower was small enough so that we could all eat in one dining room at the same time. In recent years the number of White House personnel has grown to the point that there are now two dining rooms and staff members eat in shifts. Even though I was the youngest and most junior member of Eisenhower's staff, I regularly sat at lunch next to powerful presidential assistants who explained what they were doing and why. It was a heady experience for a young man, but also an important informal network of communications for all who worked at the White House. This is no longer possible, and the increased size of the staff contributes to the lack of coordination that plagues the presidency.

Looking back on the Eisenhower staff, I am struck by the number of people who had "stepped down" to serve as presidential assistants. There were those who had been chief executives of major corporations: Clarence Randall (Inland Steel), Clarence Francis (General Foods), and Meyer Kestnbaum (Hart Schaffner & Marx). There were university presidents: James Killian (MIT), Arthur Flemming (Ohio Wesleyan), and Gordon Gray (University of North Carolina). Five former governors served on the staff. All had earned larger salaries before coming to Washington. Being an assistant to the president was not the best job they had ever held.

What is notable about the Carter aides is that, with few exceptions, coming to the White House has meant stepping up. Second-echelon assistants, often in their early thirties, make $51,000 a year. Third-echelon people, often in their twenties, draw $42,500. They may be bright, hard-working, and dedicated. But it must be difficult to tell a president that you think he is wrong if in the back of your mind you realize that losing his favor could threaten the best job you have ever had.

Another characteristic of the Eisenhower staff was its professionalism. James Hagerty, for example, was a professional press secretary. It had been his occupation since 1942. Jerry Persons, who headed the congressional relations office, was a professional congressional lobbyist. This is what he did for the army during World War II. But for most of Carter's White House staff, 1977 was a year of on-the-job training.

This assessment can be discounted as a loving tribute to an old chief and fellow workers. Certainly the Eisenhower presidency should not be reevaluated simply on the basis of how well he chose and used his staff. Still, as Ike liked to say, "Organization cannot make a genius out of an incompetent. On the other hand, disorganization can scarcely fail to result in inefficiency."

# A Composite
# Presidency

Apresidency is unique, the
reflection of a specific person at a particular historical
moment. Still, presidencies
share patterns as much as they differ in detail. In their beginnings
they reflect one another in the problems they confront and their
reactions to them. So too in their endings. But beginnings and
endings are themselves disparate experiences within each
administration, different in pace, attitude, objectives, and response.
Such observations would be readily apparent in a detailed
year-by-year description of each presidency. This sameness—the
similarity of beginnings and endings, for example—suggests a
composite presidency.

What follows is a portrait of the presidency as it appears to a
president during his years in office. At times the portrait may seem
strange, given that much literature focuses on the powerfulness of
the office. The president may seem a hapless giant, surrounded by
enemies, hemmed in by competing power centers, responding to
events that he did not create and cannot control. And yet my
conclusion is not that the office is unpowerful. But this is how the
presidency increasingly looks to the person who is president. The

From *Organizing the Presidency*, rev. ed. (Brookings, 1988).

vantage point may help to explain why presidents act the way they do.

Every second even-numbered year, on a Tuesday between the second and eighth of November, a president is elected. If he is not the incumbent, he has a period of grace until the twentieth of January during which he can organize his administration without having to assume the responsibilities of office. He brings to this task a certain knowledge and experience, and certain obligations and commitments.

If he is like most of his predecessors, he probably has a background as a legislator or a governor. If the nation has recently fought in a popular war, he may be a military man. It is possible that he has served as vice president. Some of his experience will be of considerable value: Lyndon Johnson's years in the Senate gave him an understanding of the workings of Congress, and Dwight Eisenhower's military career an understanding of the workings of the Pentagon. By the act of running for the presidency, all elected presidents should have gained some useful understanding of public opinion. But no matter how much he may have thought and read about the presidency, a new president is usually surprised to discover how ignorant he is about the *job* to which he has just been elected. Thus each new president will face a period of orientation and learning, which may take as long as eighteen months. One consequence is that a new president will make some of his most important decisions at a time when he is least capable of deciding wisely.

The White House staff will consist largely of those who have surrounded the candidate during the campaign and who have his trust. They bring to their jobs an understanding of the president-elect, loyalty, and in some cases skills such as press relations and scheduling that are transferable from the campaign. Their primary interest, however, will usually have been the art of politics, not governance. But although they are apt to begin their White House duties in a personal services relationship with the president, they will eventually acquire more and more governmental responsibilities, for presidents have a habit of giving the jobs at hand to the persons at hand. Some may be qualified to assume operational assignments, but not because they have been campaign workers. One need only look at why they were in the campaign. Often their chief qualification—

and an important one in a campaign—was availability; their chief motivations may have been the expectation of excitement, an excess of zeal, or hero worship.

The policy commitments of a new president are found in his campaign speeches, in the party platform, and to a lesser degree in the promises of other members of his party. But these commitments are usually vague, given the tendencies of elective politics to blunt the sharp edges of policy proposals. In no sense can they be considered a presidential program—a program has a price tag and relates to available resources. One consequence is that at the time Congress is inclined to be most responsive to the wishes of a president, he is least able to make his wishes known in concrete terms.

On the morning after his victory a president-elect is consumed with thoughts of choosing his cabinet and other matters of the transition. No shadow cabinet waits in the wings, and he suddenly discovers how few people he knows who are qualified to assume major posts in government. "People, people, people!" John Kennedy exclaimed three weeks after his election. "I don't know any people. I only know voters." A president-elect has political debts and obligations, but they are not necessarily to those with the backgrounds he now needs. Thus sometimes he picks incompetents. Often he turns to strangers. With each appointment, he makes a contract to share his responsibilities. If it turns out that the appointee and the president disagree, the appointee can quit or the president can fire him. Either action is a tacit admission of failure on the part of the nation's leader. More commonly, the president and the appointee split their differences and the president loses some part of the direction of his administration.

The presidential transition may be made more difficult by animosities between the incoming and outgoing presidents. The problems are naturally greatest when the president-elect has defeated the incumbent president and least when both are of the same party. Although problems can still exist in the latter case, they are apt to be caused by bruised egos rather than lack of cooperation. There will also be tensions between the incoming president and the civil service. If the newly elected president is from the party out of power, he may have campaigned against bureaucracy, red tape, and the failures of government programs. And almost all presidents-to-be ascribe an alien political coloration to the permanent government. Franklin Roosevelt considered it too conservative; Richard Nixon considered it too liberal. Nor is the new president necessarily paranoid. He is committed to change and perhaps even to reductions in programs and personnel; the permanent government may well see its interests as threatened.

The new president is exhausted from the campaign. He will undoubtedly devote some of his precious transition days to recuperating, and if he holds another position, such as governor, he will also have to wind up that business. Other chores must be attended to: planning for the inauguration, writing an inaugural address, making budget revisions, and getting ready for the opening of Congress. Government has a way of treading water during presidential campaigns as it waits to see who will be its next leader. And decisions postponed build pressure for resolution. This means that on taking office, the new president will be confronted with a backlog of decisions that need to be made. Thus is he presented with great opportunities and great dangers.

The dangers are compounded by the arrogance of an incoming administration. For two years or more the candidate and his closest advisers have been working toward a single goal, one that is incredibly difficult to achieve. Gaining it comes to few, and they have a right to believe that they have succeeded because of their skill, intelligence, political understanding, and hard work. It is not surprising that some of the greatest presidential mistakes—even those of second-term presidents—and some resulting disasters for the nation have come in the immediate afterglow of election victories, such as Roosevelt's court-packing plan (1937), Kennedy's approval of the Bay of Pigs invasion (1961), and Johnson's decision to escalate the Vietnam War (1965). Indeed, the bigger the victory, it would seem, the greater the opportunity for disaster.

The new president also finds he has inherited various organizational arrangements that were created to deal with his predecessor's problems. Each administration comes to invent offices that reflect the special talents or deficiencies of appointees, rivalries between advisers, pet projects of the president, and constituent pressures. Each president soon comes to agree with Woodrow Wilson: "Governments grow piecemeal, both in their tasks and in the means by which those tasks are to be performed, and very few governments are organized as wise and experienced men would organize them if they had a clean sheet of paper to write upon." Yet no matter how inefficiently or illogically the government is organized, there are those who like it that way. Congress, special-interest groups, and bureaucrats have grown comfortable with existing arrangements and have a vested interest in their continuation. And because the public is not usually much concerned about such bloodless matters as structural change, it is hard to mobilize. Presidents fret a lot about the ill-fitting shape of government, but generally they conclude that serious attempts at restructuring are not worth the political capital they would have to invest. Not even the annals of history reward them for such efforts. They add boxes to the organizational chart as needs arise, rarely erase existing offices unless they are glaringly obsolete, and leave government even more cumbersome than they found it.

Other elements of a president's inheritance also come into focus soon after he takes office. He finds that not until his third year will he be able to operate under a budget that his appointees have initiated. Even then much federal spending will be in so-called uncontrollable categories such as social security and not subject to his influence. He finds that his power to appoint extends to only some 3,000 people out of a government civilian workforce of more than 2 million, and because some of those 3,000 have term appointments, they cannot be removed before their time is up. The new president must also abide by laws and treaties that are not of his making. And there are traditions that he cannot ignore except at great risk, such as senators' prerogatives in choosing judges in their states. His ability to act, he finds, is also limited by the size of his electoral mandate, the composition of Congress and the Supreme Court, the rate of infla-tion, the balance of payments, the state of the world economy, and whether the nation is at war.

Yet a new administration begins in a state of euphoria. Reporters choose to be kind. Congress is as docile as the president will probably ever see it. There is not yet a record to defend. The president, for the only time, can take a broad-gauged look at existing policies. His popularity ratings will probably never again be as high. An adviser to presidents summed up this situation for Thomas Cronin:

Everything depends on what you do in program formulation during the first six or seven months. I have watched three presidencies and I am increasingly convinced of that. Time goes by so fast. During the first six months or so, the White House staff is not hated by the cabinet, there is a period of friendship and cooperation and excitement. There is some animal energy going for you in those first six to eight months, especially if people perceive things in the same light. If that exists and so long as that exists you can get a lot done. You only have a year at the most for new initiatives, a time when you can establish some programs as your own, in contrast to what has gone on before.

Then the administration has its first foreign crisis and its first domestic scandal. Weaknesses in personnel begin to appear. The novelty of new personalities wears off for the press. The president introduces his legislative program. The process known as the coalition of minorities takes hold: every presidential action will alienate someone; the longer a president is in office, the more actions he must take and the larger the number of those alienated will be. Groups that would not attack him when his popularity was high now become vocal. His poll ratings start to drop.

By the end of his first year the president should have learned two important lessons: that the unexpected is likely to happen and that his plans are unlikely to work out as he had hoped. A U-2 spy plane is shot down over the Soviet Union. Iran takes U.S. citizens hostage. There is a riot in Watts, an uprising in Hungary, the suicide of a close aide. U.S. missiles that he thought had been removed from Turkey were not removed. The Chinese explode a nuclear device earlier than his intelligence forecasts had predicted. The president finds that much of his time is spent reacting to events over which he has no control or trying to correct the errors of others.

As a result a president starts to turn inward, the quickness of the reaction depending on his personality and his ratio of successes to failures. Reading the morning newspapers becomes less satisfying. They bring bad news. They never seem to get their stories straight. Editorials and columns note only the things that go wrong. The president holds fewer news conferences. He looks for ways to go

over the heads of the press corps, such as televised speeches. He
grants exclusive interviews to friendly reporters.

Some members of his cabinet, he feels, have gone native. They
badger him on behalf of their departments' clients. Others he finds
long-winded or not very bright. There are now longer intervals
between cabinet meetings. He tells his appointments secretary to
make it difficult for certain department heads to get in to see him
alone.

Time is running out on his first term. Things are not getting done,
or not fast enough. He begins to feel that if he wants action he will
have to initiate it himself—meaning through his White House staff.
The staff grows bigger, despite early promises to reduce its size.
Types of decisions that used to be made in the departments now
need White House clearance. Bottlenecks develop as decisions for
too many agencies are funneled through too few presidential assistants. Programs that the president wishes to give high priority are
placed directly within the executive office.

The midterm congressional elections approach, and the president
tries to restore his luster at the polls. And with the exception of
Franklin Roosevelt in 1934, he always fails. His party loses seats. The
new Congress is less receptive to his wishes. As Lyndon Johnson
summed it up to Harry McPherson late in his administration:

> You've got to give it all you can that first year. Doesn't matter
> what kind of majority you come in with. You've got just one
> year when they treat you right, and before they start worrying
> about themselves. The third year, you lose votes. . . . The
> fourth year's all politics. You can't put anything through when
> half of the Congress is thinking how to beat you. So you've got
> one year. That's why I tried. Well, we gave it a hell of a lick,
> didn't we?

The president now devotes a larger part of his time to foreign
policy, perhaps as much as two-thirds. This is true even if his
interests had been mainly in domestic issues. He takes trips abroad,
attends summit meetings, hosts heads of state at the White House.
Like Kennedy, he believes that the big difference between domestic
and foreign policy concerns "is that between a bill being defeated

and the country [being] wiped out." But he also turns to foreign policy because it is the area in which he has the most authority to act and, until recently, the least public and congressional restraint on his actions. Moreover, history usually rewards the foreign policy president, and the longer a president stays in office, the more his place in history occupies him.

In a president's third year the exodus of his appointees from government begins. Many who were attracted to the glitter of a new administration find that they cannot spare any more time away from their "real" careers, especially if they come from the highly competitive corporate world. Others find that their government experience has created job offers from the private sector that they cannot refuse. Some realize they have made a mistake in coming to Washington, or their families are urging them to return home. Then too, fatigue becomes a factor. Replacing these people takes on more importance than it once had. And it is more difficult: the lure of a waning administration is not great, and congressional approval may be more difficult to achieve. The president now often turns to careerists, promoting from within.

By this time, too, personal alliances and rivalries have had full opportunity to develop within the administration. Remembering his experiences on Truman's staff, Clark Clifford recalled how "you develop areas of resistance. You come up with an idea, and you could guarantee in advance those men in government who would take the opposite position, just because you favored something." The president's needs also change. Milton Eisenhower noted that Franklin Roosevelt, in the beginning of his presidency, needed ideas (and turned to Raymond Moley, Rexford Tugwell, and A. A. Berle); later he needed legislative and political skills (Thomas Corcoran); and finally his "greatest need was for administrative troubleshooters" (Harry Hopkins and Samuel Rosenman). Rarely can the same person serve all three needs.

The president may have taken office with only the most limited notions of what he wanted to do, but by the second half of his term he has accumulated a long list of his positions, which must be promoted and defended and which will determine whether he is reelected. He now has strong feelings about what is in the national interest and what must be done—regardless of the popularity of his actions. He has come to see the national interest as uniquely his to uphold. When announcing the decision to send troops into Cambodia in the spring of 1970, President Nixon told the American people, "I would rather be a one-term President and do what I believe is right than to be a two-term President at the cost of seeing America become a second-rate power and to see this Nation accept the first defeat in its proud 190-year history." There may have been some posturing in his statement, yet it is a posture eventually assumed by all presidents. The lines harden.

As the administration enters its fourth year, the president's attention snaps back to domestic matters. The political considerations that enter into each presidential act become more determining. Appointments are made with an eye to mending fences in the party. High-risk decisions to alter or end programs may be deferred. "Wait until next year, Henry," Roosevelt told his treasury secretary in May 1936. "I am going to be really radical." Some members of the administration join the campaign staff. Those who stay in government must consider the consequences of their actions in key states. The president finds excuses to make ostensibly nonpolitical speeches around the country. By summer he is nominated for a second term and begins active campaigning.

If the president is reelected, it is largely on the basis of the past—the state of the nation during his incumbency—rather than his promises for the future. What is unspoken is that the next four years will be less productive than the first four. There are some exceptions: Wilson in 1917 and Roosevelt in 1941 had opportunities to preside over "just" wars. Generally, however, at least since Jefferson, the second term is downhill.

But first the newly reelected president will make an effort to recast his administration by bringing in new people or by giving new assignments, as Nixon did in 1973 and Reagan did in 1985. He will take advantage of his renewed popularity by pushing his legislative program, as Johnson did in 1965. He will unveil pet schemes that he had previously kept to himself, as Roosevelt did in 1937 when he proposed to increase the number of Supreme Court justices. In the president's fifth and sixth years, as in his first and second, there is considerable maneuvering room to shape events. (Although deaths and a resignation have meant that some presidents have not had their full allotment of years in office.)

Then, as Harold Laski observed more than fifty years ago, the two-term tradition (now the two-term limitation) "operates decisively to weaken his influence in the last two years of his reign. Few Presidents have had substantial results to show during that period." The president's party again loses seats in the midterm election—a signal for potential presidential candidates to start increasing their visibility. One way to make news is to attack the incumbent. The attention of the press gradually shifts to these new contenders. Some of the president's executives resign to enter the embryonic campaigns. The personnel pattern of the first term repeats itself, but it is now even more difficult to recruit from outside government. The president will continue to hold the nation's attention if there is an international crisis; otherwise, he must try to manufacture interest through summit meetings, foreign travel (the more exotic the better), and attaching himself to major events—space exploits, disaster relief, even the Olympic games. Foreign powers may prefer to stall various negotiations until a new president takes office. The last year of the administration is also an election year for the House of Representatives and a third of the Senate, with predictable consequences for the president's legislative program.

In the final July or August the national presidential convention nominates someone else. The president will campaign for the party's nominee, but it is not his battle.

After the election in November there is no longer any vital force in the administration. There is some rush to tidy loose ends. Most appointees are looking forward to new jobs or retirement. The president collects his papers and ships his files home to be able to get a quick start on his memoirs. There are farewell parties and a farewell address. The incoming people arrive for routine briefings, but except for mechanical advice, they are not really interested in the wisdom of those they will succeed. At noon on January 20 the president watches his successor being sworn in. He is an instant elder statesman.

This account stresses the institutional forces that press in upon a president. But, of course, the presidency need not be a grim experience. Depending on his personality, a president may have a very good time. The Roosevelts, Kennedy, and Reagan seemed to experience a special enjoyment in being president.

And being president need not be an unproductive experience. Each president does realize some of his legislative goals and prevents by veto the enactment of legislation he believes is not in the nation's best interests. His authority in the conduct of war and peace is substantial. Because of his position, the doctrines he espouses have a better chance of penetrating the public consciousness than the competing ideas of other politicians. His power and influence may be limited, but they are also greater than those of any other individual.

Still, the experience of being president was different from what he thought it would be or from what he learned in his civics textbooks. Four years or eight years seemed like a very long time from the outside, a very short time when he was in office. It is never long enough to do any real planning, to think about where the country ought to be, even in the next decade, and to design programs to get from here to there. The time was consumed by crises and the demands of others, bargaining with legislators, waging feuds, performing small symbolic acts, worrying about getting reelected, finding people for jobs and getting rid of them (often by kicking them upstairs), approving budgets that he could only change around the edges. He never really ran the government, as he had expected. Rather, he found that the job was to try to keep the social fabric intact; to keep the peace if possible; to defend the nation from aggressors; to maintain the nation's place in the world, even by force; to attempt to balance economic growth and stability; and at best to make some new initiatives that the history books would record as his.

# Why Great Men Are Not Chosen Presidents: Lord Bryce Revisited

On October 22, 1888, as voters were getting ready to decide whether Grover Cleveland should continue to reside in the White House or should be evicted in favor of Benjamin Harrison, the future Lord Bryce (he was made a viscount in 1913) signed off on what was to be the first edition of *The American Commonwealth*. This massive description of late-nineteenth-century democracy in the United States would have a profound influence on a generation of political scientists, but today it is recalled largely because of the name of its eighth chapter: "Why Great Men Are Not Chosen Presidents."

Although James Bryce was Regius Professor of Civil Law at Oxford when he wrote *The American Commonwealth*, his approach to his subject was journalistic, a reporting of information gathered by talking to politicians and others. As a conventional British gentleman, albeit one who loved America, he would probably have been offended by this classification; journalists were not gentlemen, of course. But in a sense Bryce was the Theodore H. White of his day, and the impact of his book was not unlike that of the first *Making of the President* when it was published in 1961. Bryce and White were fascinated by the presidential nominating process. Bryce

From *Elections American Style* (Brookings, 1987).

33

argued that party organizations generally controlled nominations and preferred mediocre candidates. Process, too, is the theme of my essay, although I conclude that it does not determine who seeks the nomination, which is now the most important determinant of who becomes president.

Although Bryce had high praise for presidents "down till the election of Andrew Jackson," he considered subsequent executives, with several exceptions, to be "personally insignificant." It was apparently the presidencies viewed up close that loomed largest on his canvas. (Even Oxford dons cannot repeal the laws of perspective.) When he first visited the United States in 1870, the White House was occupied by Ulysses S. Grant; the presidents on his next visits were Rutherford B. Hayes (1880) and Chester A. Arthur (1883). His low opinion of American chief executives, Bryce might have claimed, was based on personal observation.

Yet to have made his case for the debasing influence of parties on nominations, he would have had to prove that they pushed aside more distinguished figures. And this was not necessarily what happened. Should the Republicans have preferred John Sherman to Hayes? Should the Democrats have chosen Thomas Bayard over Grover Cleveland? There are times that seem to lack great men. Perhaps Bryce was merely observing one of history's troughs, regardless of how the candidates were chosen.

Bryce never felt the need to define greatness. He apparently thought that any intelligent person would recognize its presence or absence. This tends to turn the hunt for great men into something of a parlor game. Why, for instance, did he not pay more attention to early twentieth-century nominees? (The book was extensively revised in 1910 and 1914, with editions coming out until 1922, the year of his death.) During this period the Republicans and Democrats nominated what a British gentleman surely should have concluded were some of the finest candidates since the nation's founding generation. For sheer brilliance it would be hard to surpass Theodore Roosevelt, William Howard Taft, Woodrow Wilson, and Charles Evans Hughes. And while the populist William Jennings Bryan would not have appealed to Bryce, the Great Commoner was also a person of extraordinary qualities. All but one of Bryce's revised editions contain a footnote stating that "of Presidents since 1900 it is not yet time to speak"; still, he did change the 1910 text to read, "Great men have not *often* been chosen Presidents." (By leaving himself wiggle room to elevate his friend Roosevelt to the pantheon of greatness, Bryce also aided the cause of Anglo-American friendship, for which he had assumed some responsibility upon appointment as British ambassador to Washington in 1907.)

Necessarily, Bryce recognized that some great men would prove to be not-great presidents (Grant), and that others of more modest pre-presidential achievement (Lincoln) would become great presidents. There were bound to be surprises galore once a person entered the White House. What qualities or circumstances produce greatness is an interesting question. But it is not the question that Bryce raised or that this essay addresses.

The title of Bryce's essay reflects historical fact: no major party has nominated a woman for president, which suggests the obvious: whenever an excluded group is allowed into the pool of presidential contenders there will be more possibilities, some of whom might be great. When a religious barrier came down—with the 1928 nomination of Alfred E. Smith, a Roman Catholic, and John F. Kennedy's election in 1960—the pool expanded, but not the type of contenders. Smith, the governor of New York, and Massachusetts Senator Kennedy were professional politicians, differing from the other contenders in their generation primarily in religious affiliation. The first woman presidential nominee most likely will have been vice president, as Geraldine Ferraro, the first woman vice presidential nominee of a major party, was a member of Congress.

Although Bryce's evaluation of the American system is tinged by a parliamentarian's preference for the way prime ministers are selected, his critique cannot be dismissed as mere chauvinism. He argued that in the America he had observed, great men were less drawn to politics than to "the business of developing the material resources of the country"; that compared with European countries, American political life offered "fewer opportunities for personal distinction"; that "eminent men make more enemies" in the United States; and that the American voter did "not object to mediocrity." The heart of Bryce's argument, however, was that it was because of the party system that great men were not chosen president. Political bosses, he observed, gauged the strength of local organizations and the loyalty of voters and then calculated which candidate would add the right demographics to ensure victory. The objective was winning, not governing. He illustrated:

On a railway journey in the Far West in 1883 I fell in with two newspaper men from the State of Indiana, who were taking their holiday. The conversation turned on the next presidential election. They spoke hopefully of the chances for nomination by their party of an Indiana man, a comparatively obscure person, whose name I had never heard. I expressed some surprise that he should be thought of. They observed that he had done well in State politics, that there was nothing against him, that Indiana would work for him. "But," I rejoined, "ought you not to have a man of more commanding character. There is Senator A. Everybody tells me that he is the shrewdest and most experienced man in your party, and that he has a perfectly clean record. Why not run him?" "Why, yes," they answered, "that is all true. But you see he comes from a small State, and we have got that State already. Besides, he wasn't in the war. Our man was. Indiana's vote is worth having, and if our man is run, we can carry Indiana."

The paradox of revisiting Lord Bryce more than a hundred years after he said great men were not chosen presidents because of political parties is that political parties are in decline, and there is still no certainty that great men will be chosen presidents.

"The media in the United States are the new political parties," James David Barber has written. "The old political parties are gone." Thomas P. O'Neill said in 1986 that those who entered Congress since the upheavals of Watergate and Vietnam "had no loyalty to the party whatsoever. They looked down on it. They said, 'The party didn't elect me, and I'm not beholden to the party.'" Indeed, the antiparty feeling is so strong in some parts of the country that campaign consultant David Garth has noted, "the [political] boss is a plus to have against you."

The way presidential candidates get nominated has irrevocably changed since Bryce's day. In 1901 Florida enacted the first presidential primary law, an invention designed to take nominations out of the hands of the party regulars. By 1980 primaries selected 71 percent of the delegates to the Democratic national convention. The number of primaries dropped in 1984, but by then the news media had turned important party caucuses, such as Iowa's, into quasi primaries. Accompanied by much greater voter independence and major technological changes, notably the coming of television, the new system was expected to produce a different type of presidential nominee. Byron Shafer, a careful student of presidential politics, wrote in 1981, "Neither Jimmy Carter nor Ronald Reagan were unlikely nominees for the system under which we now choose our presidents, as Harry Truman and Thomas E. Dewey were not unlikely nominees for the system under which we once chose them."

A tenet of political science and political journalism is that as the process changes so too do the outcomes. This view is laudable and essentially optimistic. We are capable of changing the way we nominate presidential candidates, ergo we can improve the quality of presidents. Then if improvement schemes turn out otherwise, we can rail against the shortsightedness of reformers or the ignorance of those who fail to foresee unanticipated consequences—or both. The rules have affected some contenders' prospects in the past. At the Democratic convention of 1844, Martin Van Buren received 55 percent of the vote on the first ballot; at the 1912 Democratic convention Champ Clark had 51 percent of the vote. So obviously neither James K. Polk nor Woodrow Wilson would have been nominated had not the Democrats operated under a two-thirds rule, which was repealed in 1936.

But do changes in process really result in different kinds of persons seeking the presidency? Following the 1968 and 1972 Democratic conventions, party commissions duly inflicted major changes on the demographic mix and selection of delegates. Analyses suggesting that subsequent nominees were different in kind because of these changes may simply be placing too much emphasis on too few cases. After all, of the twelve major-party nominations in the past six elections, five have gone to sitting presidents. For every obscure senator from a small state who has been nominated in recent times (George Mc-Govern of South Dakota), one can find an earlier obscure senator from a small state (Franklin Pierce of New Hampshire, for example).

An obscure governor (Jimmy Carter of Georgia) can be juxtaposed against an earlier obscure governor (Alfred M. Landon of Kansas). History is wondrously full of contrary examples to confound theories.

Observing the 1952 Democratic presidential convention, the *New Yorker*'s Richard Rovere compared contenders' activities with a game of musical chairs in which each chair represents an ideological position (liberal through conservative); if a chair is occupied when the music stops, the player is forced to seek a different chair. (Averell Harriman suddenly found himself in the liberal seat, Alben W. Barkley in the conservative seat.) In terms of Rovere's formulation, when Hubert Humphrey, a lifelong liberal, entered the race in 1968, he discovered Robert Kennedy already sitting in the liberal chair and had to find another place to sit. This does not mean that Humphrey or Kennedy (or Mondale or Hart, Bush or Dole) as president would respond to similar pressures in dissimilar ways. Quite the contrary: professional politicians are more likely to have similar responses. They are not clones, of course, but they tend to weigh opportunities and constraints on the same scale. Thus some of the claims that today's candidates are markedly more ideological than those in the past may simply be taking too literally the images that contestants have drawn of themselves (and of their opponents) during recent intraparty disputes. (Reagan was one of the most ideological candidates and Carter was one of the least.) The jury is clearly still out on this question.

Following his defeat in 1984, Walter Mondale publicly worried that television had changed the rules, that future presidential candidates would have to be masters of the "twenty-second snip, the angle, the shtick, whatever it is." Having just been run over by a former actor, who also happened to be one of the great politicians of this century, Mondale commands sympathy. One could imagine Alf Landon making the same statement in 1936 after his landslide loss to Franklin D. Roosevelt, although Landon's concern would have been directed against the impact of radio. Politicians will adapt the technology at hand to their needs. For William Jennings Bryan in 1896, it was the transcontinental railroad. He logged 18,000 miles in quest of the presidency, thus ending the previous practice of candidates who stayed home and waged front porch campaigns. What is most surprising about the TV age, however, is that besides Reagan and John Kennedy, the others who have won presidential nominations are no more telegenic than any cross section of middle-aged white males. All of which suggests how little things change as the nation moves from party democracy to media democracy.

Throughout American history those picked to be major party presidential candidates have, above all else, been professional politicians. This is even more true today than it was in the nineteenth century. The reason is that "just wars" generate viable amateur candidates. Between 1824, when Andrew Jackson first ran for president, and 1892, when Benjamin Harrison last ran, persons who had been generals were nominated in all but three elections (1844, 1860, 1884). In this century only the Second World War yielded a nominee, Dwight Eisenhower. The thirty-two men nominated by the major parties since 1900 have had a collective record of officeholding that has included service as governor (fifteen), senator (nine), member of the House of Representatives (ten), vice president (nine), judge (three), and cabinet member (two). These men have moved through a maze of political jobs to reach the ultimate goal, and in ninety-two years only two members of that charmed circle—business executive Wendell L. Willkie and General Eisenhower—had never held civil public office before running for president.

To draw career histories of presidential nominees, thus illustrating the extent to which they have come from the ranks of professional politicians, is not to imply that the only way to reach the White House is to climb a political ladder, step by step, starting perhaps in the state legislature and gradually rising to a governorship or a seat in the Senate before attempting the final ascent. The ladder metaphor reflects the most common pattern, but lateral entry into a governor's chair or Congress is not uncommon. Ronald Reagan was not the first to transfer fame or wealth earned outside politics into success as an officeseeker.

With the decline of parties, it would be expected that more persons could reach elected office without serving an apprenticeship, and this has happened. It should be remembered, however, that Americans have always had what Robert Dahl called "our belief in the supposed superiority of the amateur," a belief, he contended, that "we hold to only in politics and in the athletic activities of a small number of private colleges and universities whose alumni permit them the luxury of bad football teams." Twentieth-century Americans may attribute special leadership qualities to astronauts, but nineteenth-century Americans attributed similar qualities to explorers. Recall that John C. Frémont, "the Pathfinder of the Rockies," was the first Republican presidential nominee in 1856. A journalist-celebrity, Horace Greeley, was the Democratic choice for president in 1872. Those advantaged by birth, whether an Adams, Harrison, or Kennedy, have had a leg up since colonial times. Nor did the cleric-turned-politician begin with Pat Robertson and Jesse Jackson. The Muhlenberg family of Pennsylvania, for example, sent three ordained ministers to Congress. In contrast, the businessman-celebrity has fared poorly at the presidential level, despite Calvin Coolidge's axiom that the business of America is business.

With the passage of time, what changes, of course, is which groups of celebrities turn to politics. The sports celebrity, such as Bill Bradley or Jack Kemp, is a recent political phenomenon. At least, the only nineteenth-century athlete-politico that comes to mind, like Kemp an upstate New York congressman, was John Morrissey, who had been world heavyweight boxing champion.

My point is that while contenders for presidential nominations may have to appeal to different selectors as the selection process changes, the winners to date in the TV-and-primaries era are not unprecedented in what they offer the voters. Whether today's nominees get there by climbing a political ladder or by lateral entry, they still would be recognizable to Lord Bryce. (Ross Perot would not have been recognizable, but he was not a major party nominee.) The system in Bryce's time promoted those experienced in coalition building; today's system promotes expert persuaders. Both are qualities considered presidentially important. The finite differences between politicians running for president under the old system and politicians chosen by newer rules are mainly of interest to those of us who make a living sniffing such fine distinctions.

The idea of a political career ladder based on ambition was masterfully presented in 1966 by Joseph A. Schlesinger. "Ambition lies at the heart of politics," he wrote. "Politics thrive on the hope of preferment and the drive for office." Others have since used Schlesinger's theory to show how elimination occurs as politicians attempt to move up the rungs. The final ambition, of course, is the presidency, which rises so high above the other steps as to constitute a separate ladder. The dramatic distance between the presidency and the other levels of public employment has consequences for what Schlesinger called progressive ambition ("the politician aspires to attain an office more important than the one he now seeks or is holding").

Although no person becomes vice president without being willing to become president, what of the others whose jobs make them eligible to be mentioned as prospective presidential candidates? Ordinary ambition can carry a supplicant to the level of U.S. senator or governor, but then, because of the wide gap that must be bridged, another dynamic takes over. President Eisenhower once mused that the only thing successful politicians have in common is that they all married above themselves. But the only common denominator I have observed for those who would be president is the depth of their ambition. What distinguishes the group of candidates seeking 1996 presidential nominations from other high officeholders of their generation? Not their intelligence, accomplishments, style, or the reality of their prospects. What distinguishes them is *presidential ambition*, the ultimate in progressive ambition.

In applying the concept of progressive ambition to the presidency, observers assume almost all U.S. senators would accept the highest office if it were offered to them without cost or risk. It cannot be. Indeed, the costs of running for president can be very great. In some cases the candidate must give up a Senate seat, as Barry Goldwater did in 1964. In all cases there are physical costs. When Senator Dale Bumpers declined to become a candidate for the 1988 Democratic nomination, he publicly questioned whether he had the stamina for the "18 months of 18-hour days" that presidential campaigns can require. And there are, of course, financial costs, thought to be an important reason why Dick Cheney and Jack Kemp decided not to seek the 1996 Republican nomination.

Potential candidates must also consider the almost total loss of privacy. As TV reporter Sam Donaldson noted, "Presidents must understand they live in a glass house when they move to the White House." These considerations can also have severe effects on a candidate's family. Whether to expose spouse, children, even siblings, to this ordeal could be considered the test of what divides those with presidential ambition from others who are simply eligible to be contenders. Columnist Meg Greenfield has written, "People who have made a serious run for the office or been around those that have will tell you that until you have experienced a presidential candidacy close up, nothing prepares you for the total onslaught on your life and that of your family that comes with the campaign." Mario Cuomo seemed to have all the political attributes necessary to run for president in 1988 and 1992. He was governor of New York, an office that had produced four presidents. His capacity to raise money was greater than that of his potential opponents. But he was not prepared to subject his family to "the total onslaught" and announced that he would not seek the Democratic nomination. And Dan Quayle cited similar considerations as his main reason for not running in 1996.

In an imaginative attempt to consider risk-taking potential, Paul R. Abramson, John H. Aldrich, and David W. Rohde have shown that Democratic senators from 1972 to 1988 who were proven risk-takers were "a good deal more likely to run for president than those who were not." Yet as they state in their analysis of the 1984 election, seventeen Democratic senators were "well situated" to run for president and thirteen chose not to make the race. (The percentage of Republican senators so situated who would not have run for president if Reagan had retired would have been even higher.)

This finding is in keeping with my survey of Senate news coverage in 1983, which showed that ten senators received 50 percent—and thirty-five senators received 5 percent—of the national media attention. Some of the underexposed senators were too old or too new to be of interest to the national press corps. Their time had passed or will come. But most who are rarely, if ever, on network TV do not wish to be president. Quentin Burdick, one of seventeen senators never seen on the networks' 1,095 nightly news programs during 1983, told a Washington reporter, "I'm very conscious about what they're saying in North Dakota, but not outside the state. I'm not running for president." His press secretary added, "To him if it doesn't happen in North Dakota, it doesn't happen." In any event, Burdick's age—he was eighty in 1988—made a run for the presidency unlikely.

Yet many other senators without such liabilities will never offer themselves as candidates for the top office. The Senate is their ceiling of progressive ambition. In some cases they may have judged that they are not qualified for the higher office. But mainly their reasons are deeply personal, beyond scholars' ability to measure. Strangely, perhaps, the ego strength that one might associate with a Senate leadership position seems not to correlate with presidential ambition, which strikes some leaders (Lyndon Johnson, Robert Dole) and not others (Mike Mansfield, George Mitchell).

How best to describe presidential ambition (apparently so much more intense than senatorial ambition)? William Howard Taft may have come close in a story he told about a friend's "little daughter Mary":

> As he came walking home after a business day, she ran out from the house to greet him, all aglow with the importance of what she wished to tell him. She said, "Papa, I am the best scholar in the class." The father's heart throbbed with pleasure as he inquired, "Why, Mary, you surprise me. When did the teacher tell you? This afternoon?" "Oh, no," Mary's reply was, "the teacher didn't tell me—I just noticed it myself."

Taft's gentle tale was his way of chiding Teddy Roosevelt for placing himself in a class with Lincoln (and Taft in a class with James Buchanan). But it was TR's concept of the presidency as a stewardship that separates the modern era from the nineteenth century. "My view," he wrote, "was that every executive officer [read president] . . . was a steward of the people bound actively and affirmatively to do all he could for the people, and not to content himself with the negative merit of keeping his talents undamaged in a napkin." Indeed, given the Rooseveltian way of doing the president's business, Bryce's 1910 edition deleted a paragraph designed to remind Britons that the U.S. president "ought not to address meetings, except on ornamental and (usually) non-political occasions, that he cannot submit bills nor otherwise influence the action of the legislature."

It may well be, of course, that in those days when presidents "ought not to address meetings," presidential ambition was less the force that governed the number and kind of contenders. After all, William Howard Taft did not have presidential ambition in 1908 (TR had it for him). Deeply deadlocked nineteenth-century conventions sometimes produced surprised candidates, notably Horatio Seymour, the Democrats' choice in 1868, who was so opposed to becoming the nominee that the convention quickly adjourned before he could refuse the honor. But because the old system produced more deadlocked conventions with dark horse nominees, the nominees were a decidedly mixed bag in terms of quality and should not be romanticized by political scientists and journalists who miss not having an opportunity to watch a convention of politicians trying to dig itself out of a hole. A checklist of dark horses would include Franklin Pierce, Rutherford B. Hayes, Benjamin Harrison, and Warren G. Harding.

Today, before submitting oneself to the obligations of being "the leader of the free world," one might apply the litmus test of ambition stated by John F. Kennedy, who told 1960 audiences,

> I want to be a President who acts as well as reacts—who originates programs as well as study groups—who masters complex problems as well as one-page memorandums. I want to be a President who is a Chief Executive in every sense of the word—who responds to a problem, not by hoping his subordinates will act, but by directing them to act—a President who is willing to take the responsibility for getting things done, and take the blame if they are not done right.

One recognizes the hyperbole of the moment. Still, something more distinguishes Kennedy's statement from the garden-variety ambition of most politicians (perhaps that something is *chutzpa*, the Yiddish word that Leo Rosten translates as "presumption-plus-arrogance such as no other word, and no other language, can do justice to"). Or as Alexander Haig said to the voters of New Hampshire on the day in 1987 that he announced his candidacy, "Inside this exterior, militant, turf-conscious, excessively ambitious demeanor is a heart as big as all outdoors." If this looks like a strictly contemporary phenomenon, however, consider William Jennings Bryan, thirty-six years old in 1896, a former two-term member of the U.S. House of Representatives from Nebraska, most recently defeated for the U.S. Senate, who won the Democratic presidential nomination. Or Thomas E. Dewey, thirty-eight, New York City district attorney, defeated Republican candidate for governor of New York, who almost captured his party's presidential nomination in 1940. Yes, the serious candidates are a self-anointed breed whose ambition determines the contours of presidential selection. Note, however, that not all presidential contenders really expect to get the nod. Some are in the race primarily to further policy goals or to focus attention on the needs of certain groups or to provide themselves an advantage in other pursuits. Archconservative Patrick Buchanan has contended that "there is no better forum to advance the ideas you believe in and to give them elevation." It is only the serious candidate to whom we attribute the italicized form of presidential ambition.

William Herndon said of his law partner, Abraham Lincoln, "His ambition was a little engine that knew no rest." Alexander and Juliette George wrote of the "insatiable" and "compulsive" ambition that seemed to govern Woodrow Wilson's career. Yet psychological insights cannot predict when an ambition will turn presidential. Franklin Roosevelt was said to have viewed the presidency as his birthright. But Jimmy Carter has claimed that he did not see himself as belonging in the White House until 1971 and 1972, when he met "other presidential hopefuls, and I lost my feeling of awe about presidents." Nor does presidential ambition comprehend a set of personality traits, given candidates as diverse as Eugene McCarthy and Lyndon Johnson.

Presidential ambition sets off a sort of biological timeclock. The Constitution requires that a president be at least thirty-five years of age. Realistically, candidates do not run much before their mid-forties or after their mid-sixties. Given that elections come at four-year intervals, this allows five shots at the office. At least one chance must be deducted, though, because incumbents are almost always renominated. A Republican who reached the age of presidential ascent after the 1968 election, for example, would have had to stand aside in 1972 and 1984 while Presidents Nixon and Reagan ran for second terms. Thus presidential opportunity is more like a four-per-lifetime proposition. Yet the odds are even longer in that three unsuccessful races for the nomination turn a candidate into a laugh line for late-night TV comedians. Indeed, that recent sitting presidents have been seriously challenged for renomination can be partly explained by how narrow the window of opportunity is for those with presidential ambition.

In short, contenders have remarkably little maneuvering room, and much of their strategic planning is held hostage to fortuity. Take the case of Richard Nixon, who reached the White House in 1969 via this Rube Goldberg "stratagem": (a) run for president in 1960 against John Kennedy and lose by a hair; (b) seek a way to sit out the 1964 race so you can run in 1968 when Kennedy's second term ends; (c) decide to run for governor of California in 1962 so you can promise you will serve a four-year term; (d) lose the gubernatorial race, move to New York, and retire from office seeking; (e) watch the Republican party self-destruct in the 1964 election and the Democratic party self-destruct over the Vietnam War; (f) return from exile to be elected president in 1968. (See "Nixon in Exile," later in this book.)

Unlike the lower rungs on the political ladder, where aspirants for an office have more time to wait for their most opportune moment (and may even be rewarded for being the good soldier and putting party above self), a person on the presidential track has little incentive to wait. To do so means that professional staff, volunteers, financial backers, and sympathetic political leaders will drift into other camps. A rule of thumb might be that each serious contender gets three chances and one bye. Robert Taft, for instance, sought the Republican nomination in 1940, 1948, and 1952, but passed in 1944. William Jennings Bryan was the Democratic nominee in 1896, 1900, and 1908, passed in 1904, and became increasingly implausible after his third defeat. Nor are there Damon-and-Pythias relationships in a hardball world. If a bunch of greats happen along in the same era, some will be pushed out of the way on the road to the conventions. Thus are all persons with presidential ambition generationally trapped.

This formulation does not assume that all persons with presidential ambition will run for president, merely that persons without presidential ambition will not run for president and all persons who run for president have presidential ambition. Likewise, all professional politicians do not run for president, but all serious candidates for president are professional politicians—at least until the nation produces Ike-like heroes again. It is this combination of ambition and political professionalism that limits the field in any given election year. For Dan Quayle, Dick Cheney, and others who take their bye in 1996, there will be 2000.

In the eternal search for the structural fix there are modest ways to expand the pool of presidential contenders in a particular presidential generation, such as by repealing the Twenty-second Amendment, revising gubernatorial election schedules, and revoking the constitutional ban against naturalized citizens serving as president. But under the Twenty-second Amendment, added to the Constitution in 1951, only three persons have been prevented from running for president, Dwight Eisenhower in 1960, Richard Nixon in 1976, and Ronald Reagan in 1988, and none of them would have sought the office again anyway. An additional governor or two might be encouraged to seek the presidency if they did not have to give up their state job to make the race, but there are now only eleven states in which presidential and gubernatorial elections fall in the same year. And while Henry Kissinger and other naturalized citizens (discriminated against under Article II, section 4) deserve to be treated equally with the native-born, removal of this impediment would not result in a massive incursion of presidential hopefuls. Another means of encouraging more candidacies, some contend, would be to lower the cost of running for president. The conventional wisdom—promoted by Phil Gramm—is that it would take $20 million (raised in 1995) to compete for the 1996 Republican nomination.

If fine-tuners wish to alter the type of persons who seek the presidency, the best place to tinker is the vice presidential selection process. The nomination for vice president is the single most important predictor of future nominees for president. (Half the major-party nominations for president since 1960 have gone to men who had been vice presidents.) It is a sensible precedent that presidential nominees are allowed their choice for running mate. The worst mistake a convention could make would be to pick a vice presidential candidate who did not get along, personally or philosophically, with the president-to-be.

The choice is usually a governor, senator, or House member—that is, another professional politician. The presidential candidate believes that a running mate can add electoral weight to the ticket; but in fact, John Kennedy may be the only president who owed his election to his choice for vice president in that Lyndon Johnson was the reason the Democrats carried Texas in 1960. When voters must decide who will be the next president, the candidate for vice president has proven to be a very modest influence. This suggests that presidential conventions can afford to be a lot more daring if they desire to bring new blood into the political system. One suggestion calls for presidential candidates coming to the convention with a list of acceptable running mates in a sealed envelope. The winner's list is then opened and the delegates must choose one of the names on it. (See "The Vice Presidency" later in this book.)

The fascination with process that has governed the energies of political science and political journalism has made academics increasingly useful to politicians and other practitioners while, at the same time, journalists such as David S. Broder have added a new richness to the public understanding of politics. The matter of process has consequences for the presidential selection system, and the rapidity of change since 1968 has seemingly created a series of near-laboratory experiments. By changing the composition of the convention, can we increase a party's chances of electoral success? In what proportions should parties use delegate slots to reward the faithful or encourage converts? Will an altered convention produce a different sort of platform? Which changes fuel ideology and which changes tamp it? Would presidents differently chosen become beholden to different groups and individuals? What changes increase voter participation? Has a decade of changes invigorated the parties or made them even less important in our society? All questions worth asking—and answering.

And yet in the paramount purpose of the process of choosing the major-party nominees to be president of the United States, changes in the system since Lord Bryce's time do not limit the field or alter the character of the winners. Although there are a few contenders who would not have previously emerged, such as Jesse Jackson and Pat Robertson, they have not yet been successful. There may also have been marginal or regional contenders of the past, such as Richard Russell of Georgia in 1952, who would not have entered the race today. But in broad outline, then and now, and with rare exceptions, serious contenders for the nomination are professional politicians, people of extraordinary ambition who cannot be discouraged by changes in the rules of the game. This ambition determines the number who seek the presidency at any one time, taking into account the modest room for strategic maneuver. No doubt one contender will be benefited more by a change in the process than will another, just as different contenders will be differently affected by the rate of employment and the rate of inflation. But those possessed by presidential ambition will participate regardless of whether selection occurs through a national primary, a series of regional primaries, a combination of state primaries and caucuses, or any permutation of the above.

Any democratic system is likely to produce the same range of contenders; in this regard, process does not determine outcome. A change in process may have some effect on which contender wins a specific nomination, and some presidential attributes are tested by the process. But regrettably for voters, journalists, and social scientists, the process will neither predict nor determine the chances of the winners' turning out to be great presidents.

# "Don't Just
Stand There,
Do Something"

P residential scholar Thomas
E. Cronin has commented
that when a president's poll
ratings start to drop, his
advisers always give the same advice: "Don't just stand there. Do
something!" For Jimmy Carter the advice has come sooner than for
most presidents. In the past quarter century, for those presidents who
first reached the White House through an election, the record shows
that the popularity of Eisenhower held its own after fifteen months
in office, Kennedy gained 5 percent, and Nixon lost 3. Carter has
dropped 27 points.

The first "do something" advice a president receives is to escalate
the rhetoric. Attack somebody. Congress is usually a good target,
especially if it is controlled by the opposition party. Communists
have been good for some mileage. Attack inflation, with emphasis
on greedy union leaders if the president is a conservative or greedy
corporate executives if he is a liberal. This is what William Janeway
has called "the politics of blamesmanship."

Jimmy Carter has also chosen to attack doctors, lawyers, and
government employees. This is hardly surprising. Presidents have a
way of reverting to techniques that worked for them in the past.
When Nixon got in trouble he always tried to recreate the Checkers

From the *Boston Globe*, July 29, 1978, and other papers.

speech. Now Carter has gone back to the type of populist appeals that served him well during his presidential campaign.

A president in trouble increases his public relations staff. He hires a Jeb Magruder or a Gerald Rafshoon. [A future president would hire a David Gergen in 1993 and a Dick Morris in 1995.] The basic problem, his advisers tell him, is that he has not properly packaged his programs. If only the people better understood what he was doing for them.

A president is advised to find excuses for foreign and domestic travel. Summit meetings are particularly tempting. The meaningless Glassboro Summit of 1967 raised Lyndon Johnson's popularity by 11 points. Trips to exotic places are encouraged. But Gerald Ford overused this ploy, and Barry Goldwater noted that "it would be a good thing for the country if President Ford put Air Force One in the hangar for at least eight months."

A third way to create an aura of doing something is to appoint commissions, task forces, advisory councils, and White House conferences. Carter is presently putting together an advisory council to advise on a White House Conference on the Family.

All these do-somethings supposedly have two things in common: they do not cost much and they do not commit a president to a specific course of action. But are they really so harmless? Task forces and White House conferences ultimately make recommendations. And, more often than not, their proposals will be unacceptable to the president. So he shelves them, thus heightening the public's level of frustration. The president pays a high price for the time he buys.

Nor is the rhetoric without cost. President Carter has said that lawyers encourage "legal featherbedding" and doctors "have been the major obstacle to progress in our country in having a better health care system." Yet he proposes no "anti-legal-featherbedding" program, and we are still waiting for his health care proposals. He says the federal bureaucracy "is almost completely unmanageable," but he is now the chief manager of that bureaucracy, no longer an outsider seeking our permission to set the house in order. The separation between presidential words and deeds widens.

The next do-something advice involves real or threatened U.S. intervention abroad. At least one influential congressman, assistant majority leader John Brademas, thinks "Carter's attack on Soviet and

Cuban activities in Africa might be an attempt to appear decisive in order to reverse his decline in the polls." If so, "That's a very dangerous game to play." (This view need not imply that Carter's statements are inaccurate. They can be factually correct and still be an overreaction prompted by his problems at home.)

Foreign crises, manufactured or not, are historically restorative for a president's image. Hugh Sidey, *Time* magazine's experienced president watcher, has noted that in the autumn of 1977 National Security Adviser Zbigniew Brzezinski told some congressional aides that "it might be good for Carter if he were to have a *Mayaquez*"— recalling the ship seized by the Cambodians that allowed Ford to send in the Marines. Even if Carter does not use foreign events for domestic political advantage, when presidents' popularity ratings fall, they tend to turn to the tough advocates among their advisers—the ones with proposals to do something—whether a Brzezinski or a Chuck Colson.

Some presidents' unpopularity may be well deserved. But it is not always because of the things they fail to do. History, unfortunately, rarely rewards the president who knows when to sit tight. Civics books give little credit to John Adams for *not* going to war with France. Woodrow Wilson, however, will be remembered for "making the world safe for democracy."

While doing something may be imperative, the pressures to act often mean that alternatives have not been carefully weighed. Then, too, there are times when it would be reassuring to think that presidents have some advisers who are prepared to say, "Mr. President, don't just do something. Stand there!"

# Nixon in Exile,
# 1961–1968

I should start by saying that after the Eisenhower administration ended on January 20, 1961, I had two clients within a few months, Eisenhower and Nixon. I opened a little office to provide different services for them and for very different reasons. My Eisenhower account was the result of the Republican National Committee's wish to keep Eisenhower alive politically for its own purposes. To do that, a lot of things had to be done: mail had to be answered, messages sent, and so forth. Eisenhower felt that he had earned retirement and had gone back to Gettysburg. This was before former presidents were given staffs—back then, if they wanted a staff they paid for it out of their own pocket. In this case the Republican National Committee had agreed to foot the bill for Eisenhower, so I set up a small operation and the mail was bundled up at Gettysburg and sent to Washington on a Trailways bus. We had staff who sorted it and answered the letters.

The arrangement with Nixon was of a very different type. The return to California was difficult for him. California had become his voting address, but was not spiritually his home any longer. He had

This is part of a series of reminiscences by associates of Richard M. Nixon transcribed at the White Burkett Miller Center, University of Virginia. From *The Nixon Presidency* (University Press of America, 1987).

been in Washington fourteen years as a member of the House of Representatives and Senate and eight years as vice president. Before that, of course, he had been in the navy in World War II, and when he came out, he ran almost immediately for public office. So it was very difficult for him to be back in Los Angeles. Nixon read the *New York Times*, the *Wall Street Journal*, and the *Los Angeles Times*, but he missed the feel of Washington. It was not the gossip he missed; he had never been a great gossip. He missed the touch and tone of the place. So he asked me to do a newsletter for a readership of one and describe Washington to him week by week. As time went on, I took on other assignments as well, but basically that is what he wanted of me.

I remember one thing I did just because I had the time, and it seemed something politicians might like. Each week I would gather a list of honors and events involving people who were friends or political acquaintances of Eisenhower and Nixon. If I read in the paper that somebody's daughter was getting married, or that someone received an award, I would draft a brief letter for either Eisenhower or Nixon, and they had the option of sending it. Suddenly all over Washington, I would bump into people who had received these "wonderful little notes" from Eisenhower and were intent on telling me how thrilled they were. I thought that was very nice.

In Nixon's case, I did not hear anything until he came back to Washington for the first time. In those days not all the major law firms had Washington offices. Nixon actually used Bill Rogers's desk at his law firm. We met to discuss what he wanted of my operation. In the course of the discussion he said, "Oh, don't bother to send those notes to me. I really don't want to be remembered as a person who recalls people's birthdays." What a contrast! Here was Eisenhower, considered a babe in the woods politically, yet the apolitical former president instinctively knew the utility of this personal touch. Nixon, often considered the quintessential politician, rejected this service.

That incident started me thinking, and I have never changed my view, that Nixon was a very unnatural politician. He once told me about an incident that occurred when he was a student at Duke University Law School. It was the depths of the Great Depression, during a boiling hot North Carolina summer, and he worked for a

professor who had been unable to get his textbook published com-
mercially. The professor decided to have it mimeographed, and then
force the students to buy it. Nixon's summer job was to crank the
mimeograph machine. That was before the days of Xerox, and it was
an inky, dirty job. He did it in a windowless, airless room. He
cranked all summer long. He said to me that in effect it all came
down to ends and means. The end was getting a law degree.
Anything that he had to do to get his law degree he would do. I
always thought that going through the hoopla of politics was for
Nixon rather like that.

For many politicians the gratification they get from the crowds,
the laying on of hands and all of that, really is why they go into
politics. For Nixon, it was the means to the end, which was public
service, and particularly, as it turned out, public service in foreign
relations. Somehow I think it would have been more appropriate for
Nixon to have been secretary of state and not to have gone through
this glad-handing routine. It so often seemed that his words did not
mesh with his gestures. He was not a natural politician, although he
worked very hard at politics and could occasionally be very good
at it.

When Nixon decided to run for governor of California, it was
incumbent upon me to go out there at least for several months
during the primary. I will always be struck by the ironic undertones
of the whole campaign. After all, as I just said, California was no
longer spiritually his home. When he got out there and started to
practice law, he was basically a "rainmaker," a person whose job it is
to help bring in clients, massage them, and so forth. He said to me
one day, "If I have to play golf with Randy Scott [the long-time star
of Westerns, Randolph Scott] one more afternoon, I think I will go
out of my mind." He may have used Scott symbolically, but he was
not emotionally or intellectually prepared to spend his afternoons
doing anything but talking to world leaders. Now suddenly, he was
going to run for governor of the state.

Let me say as someone who was ghost writer to Nixon, and in fact
to two other presidents and various other public people, he was by
far the most satisfactory person for whom I ever wrote. It is a very
difficult relationship, as you can imagine. Probably it can be best
described in psychological terms. Usually a person who can afford a

speechwriter has a considerable ego. But the presence of a speechwriter represents a need that the person is apt not to want to recognize. Relationships can be very strained, as many of my colleagues from other presidential administrations have told me. With Nixon it was quite different. The first reason probably had to do with his regard for the writing process. I did not work on his book, *Six Crises*, but he told me at that time that it was one of the hardest and most satisfying things that he had ever done. So he had a respect for writers and I think that was important.

The second reason was that he deeply involved himself in the process of writing speeches, articles, and newspaper columns. It was a special relationship that would tend to lead to friendships. In contrast, I can recall talking to Ben Wattenberg, who had been a speechwriter for Lyndon Johnson. He said he simply wrote the speech. If Johnson liked it, he used it verbatim, word for word, changed nothing. If he did not like it, he threw it away. Now that was not the foundation of a great friendship, but my working with Nixon on speeches was. We worked very well together.

I also found it easy to write for Nixon because he had a distinct style. I spent two and a half years as a speechwriter for Eisenhower, and I found it very difficult. I did not understand his cadence, his rhythm. Of course, it was at the end of the administration and he had had a stroke. He could not handle certain sounds as well as others. I would change the sentence structure so that he could handle the idea. He would always change it back to ways that were difficult but ways he had learned sixty years before. With Nixon, although I did not have the time to watch him make five or six speeches a day because I was busy working on the next day's speeches, I would make a point of going to at least one each day. I wanted to be sure that my ear stayed accustomed to the rhythm of his voice and his qualities. So it was a good relationship in that way too.

Nixon was generous with his praise, a very unusual quality among politicians. For instance, Jimmy Carter asked me for some help during the 1976–77 transition because I had just written a book called *Organizing the Presidency*. His secretary called me one day on some matter and said, "You know that memo you sent to him yesterday? He wrote 'Good' across the top." She did not quite understand why I was not more excited. "He just doesn't write 'Good' across the top," she explained. "This is very unusual." But Nixon was very generous with his praise.

Less important, but indicative of his nature, was that Nixon also compensated me generously. He was the only employer in my life with whom I never set a price, never had any formal contracts of any sort. The reason was simple: he would send me a check for something I had done that was far more than I would have asked or thought I deserved. I once questioned him about that. He seemed a little embarrassed and said, "Oh well, I would just pay it to the government anyway." In fact, it was his rule of thumb that on a magazine article he would send me half his fee. If he received $10,000 for a *Saturday Evening Post* article, he would send me a check for $5,000. Remember we are talking about 1962 and 1963, and for $5,000 you and your wife could take a trip to Europe and remodel your home. If I had written the article under my name, I would probably have been paid $1,000. So if I say something sharp about Richard Nixon, I do want to make sure at the outset that I have voiced my respect and debt to him for those years and my appreciation of his generosity toward me.

I think there were two reasons he ran for governor, one more important than the other. The lesser, although not unimportant for a person who was not independently wealthy—in many ways a serious problem for him—was that his financial backers told him that they could not continue to raise the sort of money he needed to maintain the fairly sizable staff of an active politician if he was not running for something. That was the nature of the game, and it troubled him. He was feeling very good about making so much money for the first time. He was proud of the fact that he was building and could afford a nice home for the first time. It was in Truesdale Estates above Beverly Hills. As an easterner it did not impress me because I did not know anything about Beverly Hills real estate—how little you got for so much. There were houses on either side, and when he put the driveway in the front and the swimming pool in the back, there literally was not one more inch of land.

But Nixon knew the price and he was very proud of his new home. The first five times I visited the house, he took me on a tour, forgetting, I guess, that he had done it already. We would stand out at the swimming pool and look across the mountains. He would say, "On a clear day, you can see Catalina." The smog was hitting us in the face, and we could not see the other end of the swimming pool; but he would say that, and I would nod.

Then one day we went there with Paul Keyes, a friend of his who was the producer of Jack Paar's *Tonight* show and subsequently the chief writer of *Laugh-In*. He was a great comic writer. We were standing there, and Nixon was telling us about what we could see on a clear day, and right next to his house they were building another house. It just had the wooden frame up, and Keyes turned and said to Nixon, "That's a lovely house, but wouldn't it be a little hard to heat?" Nixon gulped at the irreverence and never again took us on a tour. Perhaps Truesdale Estates was not a laughing matter to him.

At any rate, the first reason he ran for governor was that not being independently wealthy, he could not pay for a staff, which he needed. The more important reason was that he needed an excuse not to run for president in 1964. He needed a bomb shelter to hide out in so that he could run for president in 1968. Think of the irony of that. His thought was quite obviously that if he could not have defeated John Kennedy in 1960, he would certainly not stand a chance against the incumbent Kennedy in 1964. Understanding this, the Republican party, particularly those in it who also had presidential ambitions, would have tried to use him as a sacrificial lamb. He had to devise a way that would preempt running for president. Being governor of California, promising the people that he would serve his term, was such a way.

Although years later I heard many Nixon advisers of that time claim they told him not to run for governor, my impression was that most people told him the opposite. Among other things, because many of us were from Washington or the East more generally, or at least not from California, we grossly underestimated Pat Brown. Brown, to us sophisticates, seemed a bumbling sort. In fact, during that campaign one Sunday in the fall, he was on a program like *Meet the Press*. Bob Haldeman, Bob Finch, and I were watching it at Nixon's house. Nixon did not like to see his opponent on television. He left the room and we watched. Later he came back in and asked, "How did he do?" We had a field day. "Oh boy, he is an easy target. . . . He missed that. . . . He stumbled over that fact. . . . He didn't get that nuance right." We were going on and on when Julie Nixon came in. She had been watching in another room. She was about thirteen or fourteen. She said, "Oh, he was marvelous. He was terrific!" She saw him through fresh, unsophisticated eyes. We were wrong and she was right.

Pat Brown effectively convinced California, as he said, that Nixon just wanted to double park in Sacramento on the way back to Washington, that he was not serious about keeping his pledge not to run. That compounds the ironies, because this was one thing that Nixon was serious about: he did *not* want to go back to Washington at this point. But we could see from our own polling that this was a very effective argument. More compelling than that, Brown had been a good governor. It was very hard to build a major campaign against him. He had been particularly good on how to get water from northern California to southern California. We found one scandal of sorts, but it was so minor that it would have been ludicrous to drag out this story about some political friend of his who had had a contract to run the Squaw Valley concessions or something like that. So, in the absence of a major issue, we had to develop a collection of minor themes, which is a very bad way to run a campaign. We had to hope that the collection would add up to one major theme. It did not.

We still had high hopes, in part because our crowds were terrific, as you would expect. After all, Nixon was a celebrity. He worked very hard running for governor of what was about to become the most populous state. And the actual campaigning in a very big state is harder than running for president. When you run for president, there are many more buffers. People also recognize that they cannot go up to you and tell you their problems. A presidential campaign is on a level that can be conducted with about as much civility as you choose. You can race around the country if you want and touch hands at airports, but you do not have to. Running for governor is a different thing. The governor is everyone's person, and the state was large enough so that on a typical day we could wake up in Los Angeles, do a noon speech in San Francisco, a dinner speech in San Diego, and be back at home in bed in Los Angeles. It was a physically brutal routine.

The turning point for Nixon, as I recall, was the Cuban missile crisis. On October 22, 1962, Rose Mary Woods, Nixon, and I were in an Oakland hotel watching John Kennedy tell the nation about this most serious threat. Nixon turned to me and said, "We are finished. We just lost the election." Now election day, I think, was November 5th, so there were two weeks left in the campaign. I said, "What do you mean? What has this got to do with us?" But Nixon had a theory of peaking. Nowadays politicians use the word momentum, but the idea is virtually the same. He was building up to something, and if he got it right, he would peak on election day. If he got it wrong, he peaked before election day. He believed that was what happened—that the missile crisis was like a guillotine, a knife cutting down. With this tremendous threat ninety miles from our borders, no one was going to be focusing on local or state events. He may or may not have been right, but he was convinced.

Election day came, and I was packing my office to go back to Washington. Nixon called to say goodbye, since he doubted that he would see me that night, or have much time at any rate, and wanted to thank me. I said, "You still think you are going to lose?" "Yep," he said, "I'm going to lose." That night I did go to the headquarters, and I wrote a concession statement for him. I did not go in to see him, I just sent it in and went home to bed. I woke up at 10:00 a.m. and there he was on television marching in to give what became "my last press conference." I was shocked. After all it was no surprise to him that he was going to lose. In later years I never talked to him about why he did that. I assume it was the tremendous frustration of what he saw as the early end of a public career that came so close to the presidency.

Eventually Nixon moved to New York, which was another signal that he was finished politically. It was an era in which Americans believed strongly in having a political base, and New York was Nelson Rockefeller's political base. So there was no political motive in Nixon's moving to New York. He moved partly to get away from the fallout of the disintegrating California Republican party. If he had stayed, he would have had to spend much of his time putting the pieces back together. He abandoned elective politics for what he saw as the fast track in business and law. "Fast track" was a word he repeatedly used. For him, New York was the place where people worked harder, were smarter, and became more successful than anyplace else. He figured he would get on that fast track himself.

In 1965 Nixon and I had been on a big swing around the country for Lincoln Day Republican dinners. He always had a volunteer advance man. In this case it was a geologist, John Whitaker, who later became secretary to the cabinet and under secretary of the interior. Our private plane stopped to refuel in Buffalo; we got out to walk along the airstrip. When we came back, I said to John, "RN asked if I would join him full time in New York, and I said that I wouldn't." I had a lot of books that I wanted to write. I had been assistant to other people for a long time, and I felt that I could not make that move. John said, "That's going to change your relationship with him." I said, "What do you mean?" He said, "You said no to him." Nixon and I were always cordial after that, and I was involved in his administration, but I think John was right. I never had quite the same relationship with him afterward. Nixon hired a young man from the St. Louis *Globe-Democrat*, Pat Buchanan, as his permanent staff person.

Let me say one other thing about Nixon's time in New York, because it is a bit of his history that perhaps has not come out. In the fall of 1963 we were contemplating giving Theodore White a run for his money. He had written a marvelous book, *The Making of the President 1960*. Nixon was about to sign a book contract with Doubleday as the analyst of the 1964 election. The premise was that someone who had gone through it himself and was no longer a politician would explain to the rest of the world how the process worked. I was supposed to be the legman, organize the research, manage a staff, and so forth. We were going to meet in New York on November 23, 1963, to go over this and make the final arrangements with the publisher. Nixon was flying back from Dallas that day after giving a speech the night before. I was to meet him later at his office on Wall Street.

That afternoon I was in a restaurant in Manhattan with a Doubleday editor. A waiter came up and said something about the president being dead. He happened to have a heavy Italian accent and we thought he was telling a joke. We did not think it was funny. We went out and learned the truth from a television set in a store window. I quickly called Rose Woods and said, "What should I do?" She said, "Get to his apartment. He will be going there directly, I'm sure."

Nixon got off the plane and got into a taxi at LaGuardia. On the way in, at a red light, somebody from another car called, "Did you hear that the president has been shot?" He got home, and the doorman confirmed that the president was dead. I arrived a couple of minutes later. Nixon has said to interviewers that his recollections at that moment were of his friendship with John Kennedy, and their service in the House together. But when he opened the door for me—the first person of his circle to see him—I can assure you that his reaction appeared to be, "There but for the grace of God go I."

Nixon was very shaken. He got out his attaché case and took out the Dallas morning paper, which had a story about a press conference he had had the day before. He had talked about how the people of Dallas, when they disagree, should have respect for their political adversaries. This related in part to an incident in which Adlai Stevenson had been heckled and spit on in Dallas. He was saying to me in effect, "You see, I didn't have anything to do with creating this." He was very concerned then that Kennedy had been assassinated by a right winger and that somehow he, Nixon, would be accused of unleashing political hatred. I remember that he made two immediate calls. The first one was to J. Edgar Hoover, who assured him that to the best of their knowledge the assassin was a left winger. Nixon was, I think, somewhat relieved. The second call was to Eisenhower, who was at the Waldorf Towers; his assistant, Bob Schultz, said he was taking a nap and he would not wake him. Then we sat around that afternoon and prepared a statement for delivery before the TV cameras that were now downstairs.

The next morning on my way back to Washington, I stopped by at the Nixons. By this time the politicos had gathered. Leonard Hall, Clifford Folger, and others were already assessing how this event would affect or revive the possibilities of Nixon's running for president. But Barry Goldwater got the nomination, and his overwhelming loss somewhat cleared the Republican dockets. Some Republican leaders had chosen not to campaign very hard for Goldwater or not to campaign at all.

Nixon had worked very hard for Goldwater and Goldwater was grateful, as was the right flank of the Republican party. In 1966

Nixon did another amazing job in campaigning for a Republican Congress, and in the process built a lot of political capital for himself. Then a tumble of events occurred. It was incredible. George Romney, the early frontrunner for the nomination, said he had been brainwashed on Vietnam. And there was Richard Nixon, the man who had tried to find a bomb shelter so he would not have to run for president in 1964, so he could be the candidate in 1968. He had been defeated in California, moved away from a political base, had no national organization, and yet became a candidate and then president of the United States. It's a story of endurance, perseverance, and a good bit of luck.

# The Process
# President

immy Carter is an intelligent, decent, hardworking man. Assume, moreover, that he has appointed to his cabinet and subcabinet many men and women who are experienced and dedicated. How, then, can a president—certainly no less mentally alert than most past presidents—with many knowledgeable advisers, produce such an undistinguished presidency?

It cannot be accounted for by most of the explanations currently in vogue—that Carter is an outsider who really does not understand the levers of national governance; or that he surrounds himself with a Georgia Mafia whose weaknesses are the same as his own; or that he is a bad manager who has not been able to sort out decisions that a president must make from those that should be settled at lower levels; or that Congress is so uncontrollable it will not allow any president to exercise the reins of leadership; or that the federal bureaucracy has grown beyond the span of presidential control; or that many of the nation's problems are intractable; or even all these reasons taken together.

While there is some truth in all these explanations, I would like to put forward another theory: the root of the problem is that Jimmy Carter is America's first process president. *Process President*—using a

From the *Minneapolis Tribune*, June 18, 1978, and other papers.

definition by Aaron Wildavsky and Jack Knott—means that he places "greater emphasis on methods, procedures, and instruments for making policy than on the content of policy itself."

Carter is an activist. He wants to do things. Yet his campaign statements should have warned us that except for the emphasis on human rights in his foreign policy, his passion in government is for how things are done, rather than what should be done. He believes that if the process is good the product will be good. If he sets up a procedure for making policy that is open, comprehensive (his favorite word), and involves good people, whatever comes out of this pipeline must be acceptable (within certain budgetary limits).

A concern for process is not a bad thing. Some presidents have made a fetish of chaos in policy development, and the result has often been proposals that were not fully explored. This charge has been leveled at a number of New Deal efforts that were subsequently ruled unconstitutional. But process is only a tool for getting from here to there; it is not a substitute for substance. And good processes can produce conflicting, competing, and confusing programs.

When a president lacks an overriding design for what he wants government to do, his department chiefs are forced to prepare presidential options in a vacuum. Usually this is done by BOGSAT, the acronym for a bunch of guys sitting around a table. In other instances, when political executives have not been given some framework in which to function, they have tried to impose their own agendas on the president. Political executives and high-level civil servants prefer to be loyal to a president. If direction is forthcoming, they will try, successfully or not, to honor a president's wishes. When direction is not present, they will go into business for themselves.

Each departmental proposal—for welfare reform, or tax reform, or whatever—may or may not be "right," but there is no reason to expect that automatically it will fall into place with what other departments will be proposing. Ironically, Carter's procedures ensure that he will be unable to deal with the nation's ills comprehensively.

The Carter presidency cannot be described, as some past administrations have been, in terms of White House loyalists versus cabinet department disloyalists. In the Nixon administration, for example,

White House domestic policy chief John Ehrlichman accused some of his cabinet colleagues of going native, meaning that he thought they had been captured by their departments' constituencies. In the Carter administration neither White House staff nor cabinet officials have been given the predictive capacity that they must have to do their jobs properly. A subordinate—even on the cabinet level—has to be able to plan on the basis of some past pattern.

Take government reorganization policy. Some of Carter's actions support the concept of centralization (energy policy); some support the concept of decentralization (education policy). On what basis is an administration planner to design the next reorganization? Furthermore, uncertainty radiating from the top lowers morale throughout the permanent government and necessarily impedes the implementation of programs. Although the bureaucracy may be the butt of jokes, it is also the motor force that provides day-to-day services, and it too looks for consistent signs from a president.

American presidents have not been ideologues. And it is certainly not my vision that Carter should become one. But all modern presidents, liberal or conservative—no matter what their other faults—have had some programmatic view of government in which the specific parts usually could be fitted. This is not the case with Carter's domestic program, although he does seem to have a firmer view of defense policy (perhaps because of his naval background).

So the basic problem of this administration will not be corrected by rearranging boxes on organization charts or by doing a better selling job to Congress and the public. What has produced an undistinguished presidency? Jimmy Carter's failure to set consistent policy goals—or more grandly, his failure to express a philosophy for government.

# The Vice
# Presidency

N elson Rockefeller, President Ford's vice president,
wrote a remarkable letter, a
"political last will and
testament," eight days before his fatal heart attack in 1979. Unlike
many reformers, Rockefeller felt that the vice presidential office was
merely a "standby position." He had no patience with various
proposals to give the vice president "executive power or
responsibility in his own name," understanding full well that the
only duties a vice president should have (other than the
constitutional obligations of presiding over the Senate and breaking
tie votes) are those that a president can give, and hence can take
back.

Only the president is empowered to run the executive branch.
Beware, said Rockefeller, of all notions that could give a vice
president an independent power base. "This could create a situation
in which there would be the danger of splitting the loyalties of the
officers and employees in the executive branch." Rockefeller specifically opposed the idea of a presidential contender announcing his
choice for running mate before the national convention meets, as
Ronald Reagan did in 1976. Rockefeller thought this gives the vice
presidency more political importance than it deserves.

*Anniston* (Ala.) *Star*, April 1, 1979, and February 17, 1980; and other papers.

Yet Rockefeller's own frustrations in Washington may have led him to make too little of the vice presidency. His final assessment fails to take into consideration that four presidents of this century died in office and another resigned. It is not the *office* of the vice president that needs attention, it is the *person* who might hold the office, and thus suddenly could become president.

The national party conventions that chose vice presidents Theodore Roosevelt, Calvin Coolidge, Harry Truman, and Lyndon Johnson had their reasons, but paramount among them was not whether these men would be good presidents. Nor was this uppermost in the minds of those who gave us Spiro Agnew. Politicians want a vice presidential nominee who will help the party win the White House even though very few people vote for president because of the identity of the other person on the ticket.

Reagan's declaration in 1976 that he would pick Richard Schweiker as his running mate was also motivated by the exigencies of politics. (It kept him in contention when his candidacy was running out of steam.) On merit, perhaps, the idea of candidates' seeking the nomination as a team should not be dismissed out of hand. It fits a grander idea of the vice presidency that is now held by a number of scholars. But my own view is that it is a bad idea because it limits a presidential nominee's choice. Many good vice presidential candidates would decline a preconvention designation, including all those who have their own presidential aspirations. George Bush, for example, would hardly have agreed to run with Reagan in 1980 while he still had hopes of being in the top spot.

Nevertheless, Americans must stop being so casual about who gets to be vice president, particularly when the age of a presidential candidate is an issue. As things now stand the vice presidential selection is the final act of exhausted delegates more interested in sleep than in contingency planning. Usually they merely rubber-stamp the choice of the presidential nominee. (The last vice presidential candidate to be freely chosen by the delegates was Estes Kefauver by the Democrats in 1956.)

Two Republican state chairmen in 1980, Allan C. Levey of Maryland and A. Lynn Loew of Arkansas, came up with an interesting proposal that deserves to be taken seriously. They want each presidential contender to prepare a list of three to five potential running mates. The names would be put in a sealed envelope (rather like the Academy Awards) and the winning candidate's list would be announced to the convention. The delegates would have to choose from the list; no other names could be placed in nomination.

Under this plan the vice presidential nominee would necessarily be acceptable to the presidential nominee. This is important and quite different from another proposal that the vice presidential nomination should be go to the top runner-up for the presidential nomination. The worst mistake a convention could make would be to choose candidates who could not get along, personally or philosophically. (In 1940 the Republicans gave their top nomination to Wendell Willkie, the president of a private power company, and then gave the vice presidential nomination to a public power advocate, Charles McNary.)

Another proposal, made by a group at Harvard's Institute of Politics, calls for changing the order of the convention business. Placing the platform debate after the presidential nomination and before the vice presidential nomination would give the presidential nominee an extra day to consider the alternatives.

A more radical system was born of necessity in 1972 when Senator Thomas Eagleton was forced off the Democratic ticket, and the party's national committee had to reconvene for the exclusive purpose of picking another vice presidential candidate. Although this was never tried again, delaying the vice presidential decision for several weeks would allow the selectors, notably the presidential nominee, to focus on the options, consult with party leaders and representatives of important constituent groups, interview prospective candidates, and weigh the reactions of the press and public.

It would also allow those who seek the vice presidential nomination to appear on television interview programs, make speeches around the country, and even become the target of investigative reporters. In short, all involved in the process would have a great deal more information available on which to base a judgment.

There are, of course, situations in which holding a second meeting would be a waste of time and money. A renominated president might have settled on running with the incumbent vice president.

The national convention should have the flexibility to decide whether the second stage is needed.

In general the nation has been lucky. Several of our presidents-by-accident have been excellent. But given the current one-to-two odds that a vice president eventually will become president, some reconsideration of how vice presidents are chosen is time well spent.

# Presidential Campaigns: How Long Is Too Long?

"We're wearing people out with politics," says Nancy Reagan, who has learned a great deal about running for president in the past decade. "We'll wear the public out, wear the committees out, wear the candidates out, and wear out the press." Mrs. Reagan's husband is one of ten announced or unannounced contenders for a Republican presidential nomination that will not be awarded for another fourteen months (July 1980), and the nominee will still have to keep talking until the first Tuesday after the first Monday in November. So she raises an interesting and important question: How long is too long?

It is debatable whether presidential campaigns are actually getting longer. Before national party conventions were created, Andrew Jackson was nominated for president by the Tennessee legislature three years before the 1828 election. On July 5, 1927, H. L. Mencken wrote in the Baltimore *Evening Sun*, "The chief danger confronting the Al Smith boom lies in the fact that it started too soon." (Smith won the 1928 Democratic nomination.) And James Farley spent two years before the 1932 convention rounding up delegates for Franklin Roosevelt.

From the *Des Moines Register*, May 19, 1979, and other papers.

If Mrs. Reagan does not quite have history on her side, she clearly is on the side of the public's perception. Presidential campaigns seem longer. They seem longer because the proliferation of state primaries has made them so much more visible. When delegates were recruited privately, as in Farley's day, the campaign did not intrude into Americans' lives. And campaigns seem longer because television more quickly sates our appetite for politics, while at the same time lowering our threshold of boredom. We have grown used to stories being resolved in twenty-three minutes between and around commercials. But network news presents every evening for two years a saga of who is ahead and who is trailing.

In a free country anyone eligible to be president can announce his or her desire whenever the spirit moves, so it seems unlikely that a way could be devised to shorten campaigns. Perhaps this is merely one of those things that we will have to love to complain about.

Yet is it really a good idea to shorten the campaign if we could? Long campaigns may have a deleterious effect on the health of the candidates, one of whom will be elected president. But physical stamina is an important presidential attribute and therefore should be tested by the campaign. Running for office, after all, is not an obligatory activity in our society, and because no candidates in the past have been incapacitated by the campaigns—other than by assassins—while jet planes, limousines, and luxury hotels make the effort as painless as possible, this point is mainly of importance to collegiate debaters.

The key argument against the long campaign is that it bores the electorate and stunts voter turnout. If a large voter turnout is good, then a long campaign is bad. The facts do not support the proposition. The smallest turnout of my lifetime came in 1948 when there was the exciting and unpredictable four-way race between Truman, Thomas Dewey, Strom Thurmond, and George Wallace. There is no evidence that correlates low turnout and long campaign.

What political scientists do know is that the people who are the least informed politically are also the least educated and the poorest. These are the ones who need the most time to tune into politics and absorb the positions and personalities of the candidates. It is the best informed—the people who read the editorial pages—who tune in first, become bored, and write letters to the editor about the need to shorten the campaign.

Moreover, from the perspective of the candidates, a long campaign is a great equalizer. The incumbent president and the opposition frontrunner do not need the extra time to get better known. But the long campaign is one way to open the process to the little-known governors or members of the House of Representatives or others whose names are not yet household words.

Then, too, a short campaign would be easier than a long one to manipulate. Candidates would travel less and rely on television commercials more. It would be more difficult to separate the candidates from the images created by their ghostwriters and public relations specialists. Painful as it may be to the candidates and their wives, the long campaign gives citizens a prolonged opportunity to figure out what makes them tick. It was in this way, for example, that we ruled out George Romney and Edmund Muskie.

The present system may be tedious to observers and an ordeal to participants, but it makes considerable sense if our major concern is learning as much as possible about the person who may be our next president.

European observers have been especially critical of America's way of choosing presidents. "Success in a lottery is no excuse for lotteries," as Walter Bagehot, the English social scientist, said of Abraham Lincoln's election. The long campaign is certainly no guarantee that our presidents will be wise and able; a short campaign, however, would be much more of a lottery.

# A New Presidential Cycle Timetable

The presidential transition that takes place between election day and inauguration day is much too long. It creates an unnecessary chance of danger abroad and drift at home. Less noticed but still important, these ten weeks also may actually increase the difficulty of forming a new administration.

The most basic work of this period is to choose fewer than a hundred executives for the agencies and White House, a task that can be accomplished only by the president-elect assisted by a small group of advisers. The rest of the administration should not take shape until these appointees have been selected and can take part in choosing their own subordinates. Most of the other activities performed in these weeks amount to make work to keep people busy while the inner circle goes about its business.

To resolve some of these problems, I wish to recommend a constitutional amendment to change the inauguration date. This was done once before, in 1933, and so it is hardly a pie-in-the-sky notion.

By definition, a transition is a passing from one stage to another. Altering the transition, then, is likely to affect what comes before and what comes after. Examining transitions presents the opportunity

From *The Presidency in Transition* (Center for the Study of the Presidency, 1989).

and the obligation to look at the whole process. A very good social scientist, who became a U.S. senator, often noted that in urban policy everything is interconnected, everything relates to everything else. It is in the spirit of Daniel P. Moynihan's observation that this proposal for a new presidential selection timetable is offered.

The plan calls for elections of the president, vice president, U.S. senators, and members of the U.S. House of Representatives on the last Monday in May (Memorial Day), the swearing in of the new Congress on June 29, and the inauguration of the president and vice president on July 4 (Independence Day). Other changes in the timetable of presidential selection are also suggested.

## Election Day (last Monday in May)

According to the computations of Walter Dean Burnham, the high point in voting for president came in 1860 when the turnout rate was 81.8 percent. By 1900 it had dropped to 73.7; by 1940 to 62.5; and by 1980 to 54.3. Although most experts no longer believe that this pathetic record is caused by structural roadblocks such as registration and residence requirements that have been placed in the path of potential voters who otherwise would get to the polls, any proposal that might encourage voting should be welcomed.

Americans living across the nation's northern tier must contend with weather that is predictably unpleasant on the first Tuesday after the first Monday in November. On election day 1984 some low temperature readings were 19 in Fargo, 29 in Billings, 23 in Chicago, and 22 in Minneapolis–St. Paul. In almost all parts of the country the weather is nicer in late May than in early November. In Pittsburgh the temperature would be 62 degrees on election day instead of 45 and 88 instead of 49 in Albuquerque. There is no reason to turn the act of voting into an unpleasant chore by picking a date for elections that is bound to discourage citizens, especially the elderly and those in poor health. That people are more likely to vote if the weather is good than if it is bad is an assumption: we cannot conduct a controlled experiment in which the same election with the same electorate is held once in rain and once in sunshine. But we are not a nation of masochists, and we have the right to want to conduct democracy's work in good weather.

Holding elections on Memorial Day would be an unattractive notion to some. The idea behind the proposal, of course, is that using a day on which most people do not have to go to work could increase voter turnout. There are other ways to accomplish the same goal, however, such as weekend voting or adding another national holiday.

An act of Congress would be needed to change the election day for federal offices. I assume that states would choose to conform with the federal schedule, which is desirable but not necessary.

## Congressional Transition (Election Day to June 29)

The second section of the Twentieth Amendment would be changed to read, "The Congress shall assemble at least once every year, and such meeting shall begin at noon on the 29th day of June [presently the 3d day of January], unless it shall by law appoint a different day."

Since the ratification of the Twentieth Amendment in 1933, Congress has held eleven postelection sessions. At the last such session in 1994, eighty-eight House members and eleven senators were lame ducks (that is, they had not sought reelection or had been defeated). In the opinion of Senator Claiborne Pell, a veteran of five of these sessions, "Lame-duck sessions are nearly always unproductive, sharply criticized by public and the news media, and may result in actions unrepresentative of the will of the people."

## Inauguration Day (July 4)

Section one of the Twentieth Amendment would be revised to read, "The terms of the President and Vice President shall end at noon on the 4th day of July [presently the 20th day of January], and the terms of Senators and Representatives at noon on the 29th day of June [presently the 3d day of January]. . . ." The revised inauguration date would shorten the term of some future president, but there is precedent for this in the terms of George Washington and Franklin Roosevelt. Having five days between the beginning of the congressional term and the inauguration of the president comes from a proposal (S. J. Res. 71) introduced by Senators Pell and Charles Mathias in 1984.

Some of us still shudder when recalling the paralyzing snowstorm that struck the capital on the night before John F. Kennedy was to be inaugurated in 1961. Those whose memories do not go back that far need only read two headlines from the front page of the *New York Times*, January 21, 1985: "Reagan Sworn for 2d Term: Inaugural Parade Dropped as Bitter Cold Hits Capital"; and "Shivering Visitors in Washington Mostly Relieved on Cancellation." Under my proposal the average temperature during the 1969 inauguration of Richard Nixon would have been 74 degrees, not 36; and for Jimmy Carter in 1977 it would have been 75 instead of 27.

In addition to better weather, a July 4 inauguration day would also better emphasize the significance of the swearing in. Laurin L. Henry has written of the "rituals of democracy" that affirm the "public faith that this electoral process, despite its imperfections, offers significant choices that lead to the designation of a leader, legitimate and politically responsible enough to merit the allegiance of the entire nation. On inauguration day, personal and partisan differences are temporarily submerged; all unite in saluting the new President." What would be more appropriate than to use every fourth Independence Day to celebrate this ritual of democracy?

## Presidential Transition (Election Day to July 4)

There is some discussion in political science circles of presidential transitions as "potentially periods of grave danger . . . open invitations to unfriendly or hostile actions by other nations" (in the words of Frederic Mosher). More often, transitions are simply looked upon as periods of drift, a time when the federal government treads water despite the public concerns that require high-level attention. This is especially true when the outgoing president is of one party and the incoming president is of the other, which has happened six times since World War II (1952, 1960, 1968, 1976, 1980, 1992). For five elections (1968–84) my proposal would have reduced the number of days between election day and the inauguration on average from 76.2 to 36.2.

For two decades I observed presidential transitions from various vantage points. In the Eisenhower-Kennedy transition of 1960–61, I was on the outgoing White House staff; during the Johnson-Nixon transition of 1968–69, I was on the incoming White House staff; in the Ford-Carter transition of 1976–77, I was an advisor to the president-elect; and in the Carter-Reagan transition of 1980–81, at the behest of the Republican national chairman, I prepared a plan for transition operations. All of which leads me to the conclusion that the value of the work performed in transitions is greatly exaggerated.

About the 1980 transition, Carl M. Brauer has commented, "What residents and observers of Washington often saw was the blizzard of task forces, committees, and teams that [Edwin] Meese devised in part to reward, flatter, and occupy the conservative faithful." Transition organizations are ad hoc arrangements by definition. Yet as the apparatus becomes larger and larger, there are some who see this as an end in itself rather than as a means to establishing a more useful presidential administration.

There is an analogue in the temporary arrangements of campaign organizations out of which many of those staffing transition organizations have come. Within the transition organizations there are conflicts between the politicians and the experts, those who are there because they helped the candidate get elected and those who are there because of special knowledge of how government works. The transition organization is under added stress because many of its workers are also hoping to find jobs in the new administration. Much time is spent bickering and gossiping. Indeed the production of misinformation is so substantial as to eat into the energy of the small circle of those who really are advising the president-elect. As transition chief Meese was fond of saying in 1980, "Those who know aren't talking and those who are talking don't know."

No new administration hits the ground running. To get some quantifiable idea of how much is actually accomplished during a transition, at least in terms of selecting personnel, I added up the nominations that Presidents Nixon, Carter, and Reagan submitted to the Senate during their first month in office. There are about 500 jobs in the cabinet and subcabinet that rank in the executive schedule levels I–III. Nixon sent 85 names to the Senate; Carter and Reagan 40 each. In rough terms, then, the election-to-inauguration period produced between 8 and 17 percent of these key jobs. Since very few of these names were surprises—persons who had not been friends of the candidate, campaign workers, contributors, or previous government officials—there is no reason why they could not have been produced by a shorter and leaner transition.

President-elect Bush's 1988–89 transition had 125 paid staff and cost $3.5 million. A shorter and leaner transition would mean more reliance on the experience of holdovers and members of the permanent government. Exiting officials are usually anxious to impart the basics and the pitfalls of their jobs to their successors, even if they are of the other party. The successors are usually uninterested in learning from others' experiences. (Eventually they too become exiting officials and believe otherwise.) A shorter transition might alter this relationship, but it would not make it worse. The relationship between incoming personnel and the civil service depends, in part, on the extent to which the president-elect campaigned as an outsider, running against Washington as Carter did in 1976 and Reagan in 1980. But, as Lincoln P. Bloomfield noted, "The outsider's glib assumption that career civil servants will be disloyal to a new administration is an unwarranted calumny based on ignorance."

A presidential transition, of course, is more than a ten-week period between the election and the swearing in. Generally some transition work (though not much) is done before the election, while most of the really hard labor comes after the inauguration. A sensible transition plan, in addition to decreasing the period between election and inauguration, should aim to increase preelection planning. The problem obviously is that the candidates and their inner circles must dedicate themselves to the job at hand, getting elected. Transition planning is low priority and even may be counterproductive if it causes squabbling among the staff. The transition in 1980 produced the best record to date, partly because of Meese's closeness to the candidate. Similar offices in the future should be folded into the parties' national committees and paid for with federal funds. The inducement of public money (which would be audited and could not be used for other purposes) would give new responsibilities to the national parties. The separation between the candidates and their parties has been of growing concern to political scientists. Perhaps transition planning can be used as one way to narrow the gap.

Starting presidential and congressional terms at the beginning of summer has another benefit that would be appreciated by new legislators, their staffs, and those who would be coming to Washington to work in the new administration. The federal government would be in phase with other major employers who have figured out that this is the best time of year to transfer workers to new locations. It is the least disruptive of families, there are fewer forced separations, and children can settle into new homes before entering new schools with new friends in the fall.

Considerable criticism has been leveled at presidential selection for being too long. No other nation devotes two years to choosing a chief executive. Advances in communications technology allow us to speed up the process, it is said. The extended campaign bores the electorate, it is said. A shorter campaign would be cheaper and we now spend too much money, it is said. I am not among these critics, but I also recognize that I am in the minority.

It may be that we would prefer to hold the national nominating conventions in April preceded by the state primaries and caucuses in January, February, and March. If so, the period from the Iowa caucuses and the New Hampshire primary to the inauguration would be compressed to less than six months. It now takes nearly a year. At any rate, changing election day to late May would automatically force us to rethink the rest of the presidential selection schedule.

# Foreign Policy
# and
# Presidential
# Campaigns

"You can say all you want
about foreign affairs, but
what is really important is
the price of hogs in Chicago
and St. Louis," said William G. Stratton, the governor of Illinois.
The setting for the remark was a postmidnight meeting in Vice
President Richard Nixon's suite at the Sheraton-Blackstone Hotel in
Chicago. Only hours before, the delegates to the 1960 Republican
National Convention had unanimously chosen Nixon as their
presidential nominee, and the candidate had now summoned
thirty-six party elders to advise him on choosing a running mate.

Ultimately Nixon rejected Stratton's advice and picked Henry
Cabot Lodge, whose face was known to television viewers as the
country's chief spokesman at the United Nations for nearly eight
years. Explaining his decision later, Nixon said, "If you ever let [the
Democrats] campaign only on domestic issues, they'll beat us—our
hope is to keep it on foreign policy."

In 1960 Stratton was right, Nixon was wrong. But the evidence
strongly suggests that—contrary to the belief of many observers—
foreign policy played a dominant role in five of the seven presidential
campaigns from 1952 through 1976. One only need mention Korea,

From *Foreign Policy* (Fall 1972), and the *Wilson Quarterly* (Winter 1980).

Vietnam, the Middle East, and imported oil for America's gas pumps.

The claim for foreign policy as a crucial concern in U.S. electoral politics, however, must be tempered by four observations.

—We have not witnessed serious, responsible debate on foreign policy during a presidential campaign.

—American voters are not knowledgeable about foreign policy issues.

—The electorate's interest in foreign policy does not go beyond a basic desire for peace.

—Foreign policy issues have rarely been decisive, even though they have often been dominant.

Within this framework, a look at the 1952–76 presidential campaigns is instructive.

In 1952 the victorious Republicans, with Dwight Eisenhower as candidate, ran a "three C's" campaign—Korea, Communism, and Corruption—with communism proving the least potent voter concern. Poll data showed the Korean War looming as the most important for an increasing proportion of Americans, growing from one-fourth of those polled (January) to one-third (September) to more than one-half (late October). On October 24 in Detroit, Eisenhower delivered his "I shall go to Korea" speech, the most politically skillful foreign policy campaign pronouncement in recent U.S. history. "The origin of the speech was simple and inexorable in political logic," wrote Emmet Hughes, its draftsman. "It arose from the need to say something affirmative on the sharpest issue of the day—*without* engaging in frivolous assurances and *without* binding a future administration to policies or actions fashioned in mid-campaign by any distorting temptations of domestic politics."

Four years later in the rematch between Eisenhower and Adlai Stevenson, the Republicans changed their alliteration to Peace, Prosperity, and Progress. If Eisenhower's most important statement of 1956 was "I feel fine." Besides the question of the sixty-six-year-old president's health, the issue causing sharpest disagreement was whether to continue nuclear testing. The campaign was complicated by the Hungarian uprising and the Israeli-French-English invasion of Egypt in late October, at which time Vice President Nixon stated the case for the Republican ticket: "This is not the moment to replace the greatest Commander in Chief America has ever had."

Although questions of foreign relations—Cuba, Taiwan, the missile gap, U.S. prestige abroad—were raised in 1960, the campaign revolved around "a Catholic in the White House" and a general uneasiness among the public. "I have premised my campaign for the Presidency," said John F. Kennedy, "on the simple assumption that the American people are uneasy at the present drift in our national course . . . and that they have the will and the strength to start the United States moving again." Nixon pointed with pride to an eight-year record of national growth, but at the same time warned against complacency. In sum, Theodore H. White thought, "specifics and issues had all but ceased to matter; only 'style' was important."

The tone of the 1964 campaign was set by a Democratic television commercial, aired only once, in which a little girl plucked daisy petals while a doomsday voice began a countdown, followed by a mushroom cloud and the voice of President Lyndon B. Johnson reminding listeners that "these are the stakes. . . ." The world-view of GOP candidate Barry Goldwater was expressed in *The Conscience of a Conservative*: "The Communist's aim is to conquer the world. . . . Unless you contemplate treason—your objective, like his, will be victory. Not 'peace,' but victory." As election day approached, Johnson rephrased the question that was on voters' minds: "Who do you want to be sittin' beside that hot line when the telephone goes ting-a-ling and the voice on the other end says 'Moscow calling'?"

Vietnam dominated the 1968 election year. The communists' surprise Tet offensive increased the incentive for Johnson to withdraw as a candidate. On March 31, the day of the withdrawal, Nixon was scheduled to go on radio with his Vietnam plan. (It called for pressure on Moscow: "Without Soviet military assistance, the North Vietnamese war machine would grind to a halt.") The speech was never delivered. Instead Nixon backed off from specifics, declaring that once a presidential candidate "makes a statement indicating what he would settle for, he pulls the rug out from under the negotiators." His television spots stressed hopeful generalizations:

Video: *Proud faces of Vietnamese peasants ending in close-up of the word "Love" scrawled on the helmet of American G.I. and pull back to reveal his face.*
Audio: Nixon: "I pledge to you, we will have an honorable end to the war in Vietnam." *Music up and out.*

After a bitter split over Vietnam policy at their convention, the Democrats nominated Vice President Hubert Humphrey. Some of his advisers recommended an open break with Johnson's policy on Vietnam. But in his Salt Lake City speech of September 30, the vice president would only go as far as to announce his willingness "to stop the bombing of North Vietnam as an acceptable risk for peace." The president declared a bombing halt on October 31; however, the immediate refusal of the South Vietnamese to join peace talks left the American people confused and succeeded in neutralizing any potential advantage the Democrats might have gained. Despite the Republicans' rhetorical drumbeat on law and order, the polls showed the Vietnam War as the primary concern of the electorate.

For a time, the 1972 campaign came as close to being a single-issue contest as there has ever been, a direction guaranteed by the Democrats' nomination of Senator George McGovern of South Dakota, whose rise from obscurity was entirely based on his passionate opposition to the Vietnam War. In contrast, seeking "peace with honor," President Nixon had mined Haiphong's harbor, bombed Hanoi, and invaded Cambodia. Yet Nixon also had gone to China, held strategic arms limitation talks with the Soviet Union, made progress in the Middle East, and withdrawn more than 400,000 troops from Vietnam. Spurred perhaps by McGovern's fumbles in selecting a vice presidential candidate, the voters' verdict was overwhelmingly to approve Nixon's handling of foreign affairs.

The 1976 campaign was centered upon controversies, not issues. However, one of the controversies did concern foreign relations. "I don't believe that the Poles consider themselves dominated by the Soviet Union," President Gerald R. Ford said on October 6, 1976, twenty-five minutes into his second debate with Democratic nominee Jimmy Carter. The seemingly trivial blooper became the most publicized foreign policy controversy of the campaign, although Frederick Steeper of the Detroit-based Market Research Corporation noted, "the general public did not know that Ford had made an error until they were told [so] by the media the next day."

Commissioned by the President Ford Committee, Market Research conducted a national survey of some 500 viewers beginning that night, with fresh soundings taken at various times the next day. Some 44 percent of viewers interviewed immediately after the debate thought Ford had done a "better job" than Carter, 35 percent thought Carter had done better. By the next morning, however, Ford's 19 point lead became a 13 point disadvantage—probably the result of emphasis on the blooper in morning newspapers and television news. The gap widened to 26 percent during the afternoon. The October 7 evening interviewing, which extended beyond the evening news, showed the largest change: 61 percent of those interviewed now thought Carter had won the debate.

Ultimately, the burden of Watergate proved too great for Ford, an appointed president, and the voters narrowly chose a Democrat whose principal campaign theme was that he did not have any Washington experience.

Clearly, in most of these campaigns foreign policy as a matrix of issues boiled down to who was most apt to get or keep us out of war. Highly technical matters such as international finance or even explosive situations that were unlikely to involve American troops were not the stuff on which electoral mandates were constructed.

It is Daniel P. Moynihan's widely shared opinion that "elections are rarely our finest hour." In a political campaign, issues are always oversimplified, overdramatized, and overcatastrophized. Perhaps in practice there should be no expectation that presidential campaigns will be appropriate vehicles for objective, thorough, balanced reviews of public policy. Although this observation applies to both domestic and international issues, the latter are made even more inscrutable by their complexities, secrecy restrictions, and the limited knowledge of most voters. Thus it can be stated as a general law of campaigning: *all issues are handled badly, but foreign policy issues are handled worst.*

The electorate's ignorance of issues is probably the most thoroughly documented finding in surveys of voter behavior. In 1964 a survey by University of Michigan researchers found that 28 percent of those interviewed did not know there was a communist regime in

China. A majority (three out of five) of those who voted for Eugene
McCarthy in the 1968 New Hampshire Democratic primary probably did not know that the Minnesota senator was a dove on the
Vietnam War because they considered the Johnson administration as
not hardline enough and may have failed to see the difference
between the two.

Still, as political scientist V. O. Key pointed out, "voters are not
fools." In 1960, for example, Nixon received 59 percent of the
African-American vote in Atlanta; in 1964 Goldwater received less
than 1 percent of that vote. Many of these voters may not have
known the substance of the Civil Rights Act of 1964 or that
Goldwater voted against it, but their massive vote shift suggests that
they had a firm idea of which candidate would be most sympathetic
to their interests.

About a third of the voters probably make up their minds before
the conventions, another third during the conventions, and the rest
during the campaign. Many U.S. presidential elections are close
enough for the time between the conventions and election day to
make a difference in the outcome. During this period, the only
determinants of voting that the candidates can manipulate are "the
issues"—what they choose to stand for or ignore. And it is here that
the candidates have emphasized foreign policy.

These issues have not necessarily been decisive in terms of outcomes; they have merely been dominant, as selected by the candidates from a range of potential options. With pristine hindsight, it is
obvious that whether the candidates debated the need for acquiring
more nuclear weaponry (which they did) or the low price of hogs
(which they did not), Eisenhower would have been given a second
term and Goldwater would have been decisively defeated. In 1952
and 1968, the poll takers tell us, lack of progress in ending the wars
in Korea and Vietnam, respectively, was a compelling component of
the voters' "time for a change" decisions rather than isolatable causes
for the Republican victories.

Given, however, that the electorate has less interest in and less
knowledge of foreign relations than of domestic affairs, it is clear that
on the international issues the voters do care about, they care very
deeply indeed. Foreign policy becomes a dominant campaign issue
only when it has reached the raw nerve of the electorate and is thus

domesticated in the sense of being brought home. American actions on matters of great importance, often relating to world economic conditions, may affect almost no votes at all. They have not reached that raw nerve. But U.S. policy vis-à-vis some countries has become so domesticated that both parties must pay special attention to them at all times. The "three-I circuit"—Italy, Ireland, Israel—was long a standard itinerary for American politicians; and Israel, in particular, gets special attention in candidates' campaign rhetoric, including promises to move the American embassy to Jerusalem.

Candidates' appeals concerning international affairs are basic, even primitive. "I have said this before, but I shall say it again and again and again: Your boys are not going to be sent into any foreign wars" (Franklin Roosevelt, 1940). "If there must be a war there in Korea, let it be Asians against Asians. . . ." (Dwight Eisenhower, 1952). "We are not about to send American boys 9 or 10,000 miles away from home to do what Asian boys ought to be doing to protect themselves" (Lyndon Johnson, 1964).

Given two factors that have worked powerfully to keep foreign policy discussions out of election year debates, the quantity if not the quality of these debates has been noteworthy. First, there has been the pervasive underlying American belief that "politics stops at the water's edge," that extreme partisanship is not only out of place with respect to foreign affairs but also somehow un-American. Massive disillusionment with the 1965–73 Vietnam involvement eroded this feeling, but candidates still find it necessary to pay lip service to it. As the veteran reporter Merriman Smith commented, "Consider the number of times in 1968 that one candidate or another was heard to say that he did not intend to trifle with national interests by making the war in Vietnam a political issue. Then, for the next 15 minutes he usually talked about Vietnam and the unrealistic, immoral, or misguided position of the other candidates." Second, issues tend to surface in American politics because of strong prompting from pressure groups, which traditionally are organized along occupational lines. Labor unions, the American Medical Association, and farm groups, for instance, may have positions on international relations, but these positions are not generally central to their purposes.

Ethnic groups, of course, often feel very strongly about U.S. policies abroad. Irish-Americans and German-Americans lobbied to prevent U.S. intervention in both world wars. Predictable pressure has come from East European (anti-Soviet) and Jewish (pro-Israeli) groups and, more recently, from Greek (anti-Turkish) and black (anti–South African) spokesmen. Some 12,000 blacks marched to the Washington Monument—renamed Lumumba Square for the day—in May 1972, where Congressman Charles Diggs told them that it is "time for people in America and the Caribbean to see that our African past is connected to the African future. . . . We are sounding a warning that no longer will the movement for justice stop at the water's edge." Yet on the scale of forces that weigh most heavily in the making of presidential election issues, these are modest, although not inconsequential.

An important reason for the prominence of foreign policy in recent presidential politics is that it has most engaged those who by some mysterious process become labeled in the press as "potential presidential nominees." More of this breed, including John Kennedy, Hubert Humphrey, Eugene McCarthy, Edmund Muskie, Joseph Biden, and Richard Lugar, have served on the Foreign Relations Committee than on any other single Senate committee.

Eisenhower, of course, came from the military, but with assignments that heavily involved international diplomacy. Nixon's foreign relations experience went back to membership on a 1947 House committee that prepared a key report on aiding postwar Europe. McGovern had been Food for Peace director; his ultimate running mate, Sargent Shriver, had been Peace Corps director. Even many of the governors whose names have been in that magic circle of potential presidents have had some foreign policy experience— Stevenson, Averell Harriman, Nelson Rockefeller, and William Scranton. And those governors without a background in foreign affairs usually have tried to simulate this experience through overseas trade missions and membership on such bodies as the Trilateral Commission, as did Jimmy Carter.

Moreover, foreign policy has occasionally become an issue in presidential campaigns because the candidates have wished it to be, because it was the area in which they were most interested. Take the case of Adlai Stevenson in 1956. Well before the convention, Stevenson's advisers reached the conclusion, based on a detailed study of voter attitudes and public opinion polls, that the Democratic campaign should be waged on domestic policy. "Concentrating on domestic issues," wrote Arthur Schlesinger, Jr., and Seymour Harris, two members of the candidate's braintrust, "would renew the image of the Democratic party as the people's party, leading the nation out of depression and poverty, while too much talk about foreign policy might simply remind people that the nation had been at war several times when Democratic administrations were in power." The Stevenson offensive was to be called the New America—a phrase he used in accepting the nomination—and would emphasize such matters as education, medical care, civil rights, civil liberties, and the problems of children and the aged.

But as the campaign proceeded the candidate became increasingly restless with this strategy. By late October he was telling audiences, "I want to talk with you about the most serious failure of the Republican administration. I mean its failure in conducting our foreign policy." And so the New America fell into disuse as Stevenson fought his lost cause over terrain on which he knew himself to be at a decided disadvantage but to which he seemed magnetically attracted.

The primary issue on which Stevenson challenged the president was hydrogen bomb testing: Stevenson believed testing should be suspended; Eisenhower did not. The discussion was largely free of acrimony and innuendo. Rarely has an American election produced two candidates so intolerant of demagoguery and political overkill. It is instructive, however, as an example of how badly matters of such complexity are handled under the best of circumstances, how befuddled it left the voters and how little it influenced the canvass.

The two candidates differed sharply on whether nuclear weapons policy was a proper subject for a campaign airing. Stevenson said, "I have chosen to make this proposal for peace a political issue. But I think this is good. After all, the issue is mankind's survival, and man should debate it, fully, openly, and in democracy's established processes." Eisenhower replied, "I regret this fact. The manner in which the issue has been raised [that is, in a political campaign] can lead only to confusion at home and misunderstanding abroad. . . . This specific matter is manifestly not a subject for detailed public discussion—for obvious security reasons."

Both candidates were partly right (or partly wrong). In retrospect, one could say that the American people were given some useful information with some clear differences between the candidates. They were also given conflicting scientific evidence that could "lead only to confusion" and some gaps in information for "security reasons."

Even in the hands of such honorable men as Stevenson and Eisenhower the discussion contained distortion. Stevenson changed his position in mid-passage. On April 21, he had said, "We should give prompt and earnest consideration to stopping further tests of the hydrogen bomb." By the end of October he was contending, "I have never proposed the prohibition of tests of other than large H-bombs." Eisenhower issued a ten-point statement on "the government's policies and actions with respect to the development and testing of nuclear weapons." Stevenson responded selectively to half the points; Eisenhower responded not at all to some of Stevenson's arguments.

In a narrow sense, the point at issue boiled down to Stevenson's contention that the United States should unilaterally stop testing large H-bombs and Eisenhower's contention that it should not. But more broadly the contenders were off on different tracks. Stevenson's concern was with what his opponent called "the lesser matter of the testing of our nuclear weapons"; Eisenhower's concern was with the general question of disarmament: "The critical issue is not a matter of testing nuclear weapons," he said, "but of preventing their use in nuclear war." The issue, the most important substantive one of the campaign, was simply never joined. As is always the case, it was not equally in the candidates' interests to meet the opposition on common ground. They did not, and there was no force or mechanism to hold them accountable.

If the 1956 exposition of nuclear policy illustrates what one can expect of serious campaign discussion at its "best," the same issue in 1964 shows how deep is the abyss into which presidential politics can descend. To understand how the 1964 campaign could have turned into "a steady diet of horror stories" (Republican strategist Stephen Shadegg's phrase), it is necessary to recall that at the time of his nomination Barry Goldwater was a member of the Senate Armed Services Committee, a member of the Preparedness Investigating Subcommittee of the Armed Services Committee, a member of the Appropriations Subcommittee on the Department of Defense, a

member of the Appropriations Subcommittee on Military Construc-
tion, and a major general in the air force reserves. Goldwater was
fascinated by and possessed a good deal of information on the
technicalities of U.S. defense posture. It was his attempt to translate
these technicalities into the idiom of political discourse that led to his
image as "a nuclear bomber."

In the hands of a candidate with greater finesse, the problem of
how to turn the average voter into an instant expert on military
hardware and strategy still would have remained. The Republican
nominee seemed to view the campaign primarily as "an educational
process," although its unsuitability for this purpose has been repeatedly illustrated.

Take Goldwater's "nuclear defoliation" proposal. The following
exchange is from ABC-TV's *Issues and Answers* on May 24, 1964:

> Howard K. Smith: "Now, a lot of the supply lines seem to run
> in on the Laotian border, in any case through jungles and long
> trails. How could you interdict those? There's no good. . . ."
> Goldwater: "Well, it's—it's not as easy as it sounds because
> there aren't trails that are out in the open. I've been in these
> rain forests of Burma and south China. You're perfectly safe
> wandering through them as far as an enemy hurting you. There
> have been several suggestion made. I don't think that we
> would use any of them, but defoliation of the forest by low-
> yield atomic weapons could well be done. When you remove
> the foliage you remove the cover."

Three days later at a Los Angeles press conference Goldwater tried
to clarify his statement:

> the fact of the matter is that I—in answer to the question, a
> technical question, not a question of what would you do but a
> question of how could it be done, and mind you this question
> has been discussed and discussed and discussed by the military
> and by its study groups all over this country. I can't reveal the
> nature of them because they're highly classified. But I was
> merely answering a question put to me in a decent way by a
> news commentator and I recognized at the outset that we

wouldn't use them, I never have advocated it, I don't advocate it now. But times might change. I don't think they will, I think we can stop those supplies without resorting to that, I was merely answering a question.

Goldwater was right, of course: It was possible—militarily—to defoliate forests; he had not advocated it. Or had he? "But times might change," he said. And why was he talking about such nuclear possibilities at all, especially if he opposed them? Smith had not asked him specifically about defoliation; and even if he had, that was hardly a sufficient reason in politics.

From such remarks, it was only a natural political progression to the Rockefeller mailing ("Who Do You Want in the Room with the H-bomb?") that went out to 2 million registered Republicans in the crucial California primary to Scranton's open letter to Goldwater at the convention ("You have too often casually prescribed nuclear war as a solution to a troubled world") to the TV spot of the girl with the daisy.

On a wide range of issues, foreign and domestic, Goldwater had delivered on his promise to offer the voters "a choice, not an echo." But it takes two to debate. And Johnson preferred to ignore his opponent's arguments; to have done otherwise would have both advertised them and lent respectability to them. The purpose of an election campaign in the American political tradition is not to arrive at the truth, but to win. For Johnson (as it had been for Rockefeller and Scranton), the temptation was irresistible to turn Goldwater's statements into emotionally charged shorthand. Moreover, in focusing on nuclear weapons policy, often in a crude manner, Goldwater evoked the sorts of images that do not contribute to enlightened electioneering. "You mention the word nuclear," he was to remark later, "and all they can think of is the big mushroom cloud, the red blast and twenty million dead."

Questions of nuclear policy, as aired by Stevenson and Eisenhower in 1956, Barry Goldwater in 1964, and George Wallace's running mate, Curtis LeMay, in 1968, show how ill-suited matters of high complexity and technical content are to discussion in a presidential campaign. Two other matters, raised in 1960—the possibility of a "missile gap" between the United States and the Soviet

Union and what was to be done about Fidel Castro's communist takeover of Cuba—illustrate the problems of debating issues that are shrouded in official secrecy.

Following the successful Soviet missile tests of 1957, the matter of the relative missile production of the two superpowers moved in glacieresque fashion from discussions in the Pentagon to debate in Congress to campaign topic, gathering momentum year by year, while losing those rough edges of doubt, detail, and perspective that would have slowed its descent into political rhetoric.

By 1959 the issue had been expropriated from the generals by Senator Stuart Symington, a former secretary of the air force, and, more important at the time, a potential Democratic candidate for president. The senator charged that Soviet capabilities would shortly give them a three-to-one lead over the United States in intercontinental ballistic missiles and that "the intelligence books had been juggled so that the budget books may be balanced." Eisenhower's defense secretary, Thomas Gates, responded that "there is no *deterrent* gap."

During the fall campaign against Nixon, Kennedy did not stress the missile gap, although it was a part of his stump vocabulary: "The Republican party, the same party which gave us the missile gap. . . . "(Minneapolis, October 1); "I have confidence in our ability to close the missile gap. . . ." (St. Louis, October 2).

Less than a month after Kennedy's inauguration, Defense Secretary Robert S. McNamara, now privy to the appropriate classified documents, announced to a press conference that there was no missile gap, although his remarks were officially "not for attribution." By Thanksgiving, word was out that Kennedy too had formally buried the issue. This explanation must have been cold comfort for Richard Nixon. In an analysis of 1956–60 voters who switched from one party to the other, James Sundquist concluded that the second most helpful issue for the Democrats was the missile gap (after unemployment).

The Cuban issue was raised by John Kennedy in a surprisingly militant statement on October 20, 1960: "We must attempt to strengthen the non-Batista democratic anti-Castro forces in exile, and in Cuba itself, who offer eventual hope of overthrowing Castro. Thus far these fighters for freedom have had virtually no support from our government." What Kennedy had proposed, in effect, was the covert CIA operation then in preparation that would ultimately be transformed into the Bay of Pigs invasion. Nixon, who had been the project's advocate within high administration councils, thought that Kennedy had been briefed on the plans and, as he wrote later, was privately furious at his opponent for "jeopardizing the security of a United States foreign policy operation."

The day after Kennedy's statement the two candidates met for their final TV debate. When the question of the Cuba proposal was raised, Nixon attacked:

> If we were to follow that recommendation . . . we would lose all of our friends in Latin America, we would probably be condemned in the United Nations, and we would not accomplish our objective. . . . It would be an open invitation for Mr. Khrushchev . . . to come into Latin America and to engage us in what would be a civil war and possibly even worse than that.

Nixon was to explain later that this tack was the "only thing I could do. The covert operation had to be protected at all costs. I must not even suggest by implication that the United States was rendering aid to rebel forces in and out of Cuba. In fact, I must go to the other extreme: I must attack the Kennedy proposal to provide such aid as wrong and irresponsible because it would violate our treaty commitments."

Whether this was the only thing that Nixon could have done is a moot question. The point is that a responsible candidate will engage in what politicians call honest lying to maintain national security secrecy. But for voters who are prayerfully trying to weigh the merits of each issue, they must somehow factor in the possibility that what they are being told is not true. So secrecy becomes another roadblock in the path of rational campaign rhetoric. One more puzzlement: Had the Republican party won in 1960, Douglass Cater writes, "how Nixon as President would have dealt with the C.I.A. operation he so vigorously denounced remains to be speculated."

Nixon's dilemma over what to say about U.S. plans for Cuba suggests the liabilities of incumbency. Yet, on balance, the advantages of incumbency in dealing with foreign policy in a presidential campaign are substantially greater. At its most elemental, how does one measure the worth to President Franklin Roosevelt, the wartime commander-in-chief, of opening his 1944 campaign for reelection from the deck of a navy destroyer, its guns as background, as thousands of shipyard workers lined the docks of Bremerton, Washington, and millions more listened over nationwide radio? Or what better exit line can one imagine than President Lyndon Johnson, after Khrushchev was ousted in the midst of the 1964 campaign, saying to reporters, "I'm sorry I can't stay around and talk with you—[Soviet] Ambassador Dobrynin is coming over to see me."

To run against a president is to live in constant terror of being upstaged. Will unexpected world events, such as Khrushchev's fall from power in 1964, give the incumbent an opportunity to play statesman while all around him are merely office seekers? Will a last minute crisis, as in the Soviet invasion of Hungary in 1956, produce a rally-round-the-president response among the voters?

While the president has less than total control over the world situation, his opponent has none. Johnson's request for the Tonkin Gulf resolution in August 1964 boosted his rating on "handling Vietnam" in the Harris poll from 42 percent to 72 percent. After meeting with visiting Soviet Premier Alexei Kosygin in 1967, Johnson's popularity jumped 11 points, although a majority of those interviewed did not believe that the Glassboro, New Jersey, summit "brought peace closer" and only 19 percent thought the meetings would help settle the Vietnam War. In the collective public mind, the president was aided by an action that was largely perceived as useless, but at least he had done something.

If the incumbent seeking reelection also happens to be a Republican, the odds rise measurably that he will try to keep the campaign focused on foreign policy. Among those who see a difference between the parties' capacities to handle foreign policy, the balance of expectations favored the Republicans by more than five to one in 1956 and two to one in 1960 and 1968. (Only in the Goldwater campaign was the margin reversed in favor of the Democrats.) And a simulation of the 1960 election by MIT political scientists contended that Nixon would have won easily if the campaign had been riveted on foreign policy issues.

Of course the timing of foreign crises becomes a matter of some moment. The Tet offensive, coming in January of 1968, knocked Johnson out of the race. Would it have elected him if it had come in October? The existence of a volatile international situation during the fall campaign worked to the advantage of the party in power (1956); a period of peaceful calm did not (1960).

There are no changes in the geography or the geometry of American politics to suggest that foreign policy issues are less likely to be raised in future presidential races. Or that they will be handled more responsibly than in the past. On the contrary. One development suggests that all issues—domestic and international—will be handled with more heat and less light. Political parties traditionally have represented so many different interests that each interest group has had to make compromises in order to remain within the party. The parties, in other words, have long tended to mute intensity on any given issue. Thus the steady decline of the parties has serious consequences. The current disarray of the Democratic party, for instance, removes some of the pressure for consensus that has long held in balance the basic interests of organized labor, blacks, and Jews. Each group now has less incentive to act in tandem.

The irony is that the foreign policy promises the candidates make probably have little to do with the foreign policy crises that presidents actually confront. Judging from recent history, voters would be better served if candidates addressed such questions as: What would you do if a hostile power put offensive missiles in Cuba? How would you react if North Korea invaded South Korea? Unfortunately contenders for the presidency do not answer hypothetical questions. But if they did, the results would be more interesting—and certainly more useful—than the foreign policy debates that now erupt in presidential campaigns.

# Throw the
# Rascals Out

Before we again become too high-minded about the failure of presidential campaigns to map future public policy and ingest many more editorials about the absence of elevated discourse, let us remind ourselves what American electoral politics is about.

Throughout U.S. history getting elected has been the candidates' priority. This is no sudden mid-twentieth-century phenomenon. It was as true of Abraham Lincoln as it is of Ronald Reagan. The Lincoln who had debated Stephen Douglas, when accepting the 1860 Republican nomination, asked his supporters to "kindly let me be silent." Occasionally politicians will wage a campaign of "great issues," but you can be sure it is because they cannot avoid them or feel that such conduct is in their best interests.

Though the reasonable discussion of issues is "the dream of unblooded political scientists," as Theodore White has said, the electorate still receives a huge quantity of information that is useful in making a decision. The information is largely negative. The contenders try to prove that the incumbents have failed; the incumbents accuse contenders of being incompetent or dangerous. Because this is not uplifting, we often disparage its importance.

From the *San Diego Union*, October 5, 1980, and other papers.

The elemental function of an election is to provide for a plebiscite on the conduct of the person in power. Whenever a president is running for reelection, the basic question always will be: Do you approve of what has been done to you or for you during the past four years? Assuming that a reelection promises more of the same, the question is far from irrelevant. The option is whether to retain or reject. An election is more clouded when none of the candidates is an incumbent, as in 1952, 1960, and 1968. But the president's party is always on the ballot, and these elections illustrate how the voters exercise rejection politics even when a president is not running.

Thus every presidential election is a blunt yet efficient instrument. Not a just instrument. A president and his party are blamed for everything that happens while they are in office, whether or not they are at fault. (They also try to take credit beyond what they are entitled to.) Nevertheless, there is a certain raw logic in using elections as a way to reckon with the past. That Herbert Hoover did not create the Great Depression hardly negated the argument that it was time for a change. Or, as a worker at B. F. Goodrich in Akron recently said, "It's never been this bad before, and someone has to be held accountable." Elections, rightly, are about accountability.

Elections, then, are guaranteed opportunities to throw the rascals out. We would like to know, of course, whether the alternatives are going to be worse rascals, but this is a much more difficult question. There are no schools in which contenders' aptitudes can be graded, nor are there even agreed-upon measurements for predicting presidential performance. Recall that Walter Lippmann, during the 1932 campaign, wrote of Franklin D. Roosevelt, the Democratic nominee: "He is a pleasant man, who without any important qualifications for the office, would very much like to be President. . . . The judgment has formed itself among large numbers of discerning people that here is a man . . . who simply does not measure up to the tremendous demands of the office of President." So spoke our greatest twentieth-century journalist of the man who would prove to be our greatest twentieth-century president. An irony is that Hoover, the incumbent, had a pre-presidential record of exceptional quality. In 1932 the voters rejected Hoover, the brilliant failed president; in 1936 they retained Roosevelt, by then an unqualified success. This is what elections do with exquisite finality.

It is perhaps therapeutic and otherwise useful to bemoan what elections do not do, but before utter disillusion sets in, a reminder of what the presidential campaign is about is in order.

# Presidential Policy: Making It Happen

There is no shortage of proposed policies and programs from which a new president can choose. Their excellence alone will not make them happen. Making them happen depends on the skill of the assistants and advisers the president appoints, the paths he picks for their realization, and the way he relates to the press and the public, among other factors. Happening is the focus of these thoughts, which are intended for a first-year president who wants to be reelected. (It is likely that a president who decides—but does not announce—that he is not going to seek reelection would conduct himself differently. Because second terms are always downhill anyway, unless there is a great war or depression, this notion is worth examining sometime.)

As Richard Nixon was about to take office in 1969, his speechwriter Raymond Price sent him a memo. "For a third of a century, the fashionable critics have been measuring progress according to the standards established by [Franklin] Roosevelt in his first 100 days," Price wrote. "If we're going to change the pattern of government, we've got to change the standards of measurement."

From *Critical Choices* (Brookings, 1989).

Doing away with this accent on hundred days—what Price called the "frenzies of activity for activity's sake"—is the consummate good-government proposal. A new president deserves time to take stock of the executive branch, choose personnel, and design a legislative program. Price's advice is not wrong, but no president can afford to follow it. Presidents no longer have the luxury of settling in.

The logic of the hundred days strategy is that presidents can get things from Congress and others that will not be forthcoming later. The good will and fair play accorded a newly franchised presidential team do not last long. A president must grab the chance when it comes around. But the overriding reason for a fast start is not directly related to a president's so-called honeymoon period. Rather, the attention of the public and the attitude of the media are such that a president initially is noticed in a way that is unlikely to happen again. What a president does in his first few months in office is apt to cast his image in a mold that is extraordinarily difficult to alter. The public perceptions of the Carter and Reagan presidencies became firmly fixed in the first year, even though historians may prove that those early impressions were not accurate portrayals of those presidents' time in office. President Clinton's choosing to start his administration with a directive condoning gays in the military also had consequences for public perception that were beyond the issue at hand.

A president-elect might once have been advised to take his lumps early. Such advice has now been replaced by a new adage: have a decisive victory, then take your lumps. Indeed, a new president who comes to office without a complete program should promptly develop a limited agenda designed to produce at least one early victory. Presidents do have accomplishments after the first year, but those achievements may be cold comfort when they run for reelection. In electoral terms, then, getting off to a fast start is imperative.

The fast-start strategy calls into question the value of a multiple-advocacy staff system in which the clash of competing ideas promises to produce a well-tested policy. The more opinions, conflicting or otherwise, a president is given, the longer a decision will take. Richard Nixon did not announce his domestic program until August of his first year. His advisers did not lack energy and talents. The problem was the president's system of multiple advocacy. The tug-of-war between Daniel P. Moynihan and Arthur Burns, resident scholars on the White

House staff, ultimately mediated by John Ehrlichman and George Shultz, was not resolved for more than six months. Although adequate attention and staff given to developing alternative proposals helps avoid mistakes, a president cannot wait for the perfect proposal any more than a surfer can wait for the perfect wave.

Every incoming president vows that he will not make the same errors as the outgoing president. That the outgoing executive has made mistakes is a given. That new presidents judge they have a mandate to be different is also a given. This drive to be different is most obvious if the new administration is of a different political party than the old administration, especially if an incumbent president has been defeated. But the urge to start afresh is present even when the new president is the old vice president.

The principle of contrariness is very strong. But after newly installed President John Kennedy disbanded predecessor President Dwight Eisenhower's National Security Council machinery, he was left without a proper advisory body in the White House during the Bay of Pigs crisis. Jimmy Carter's antipathy to having a chief of staff, which dissipated his administration's efficiency, was partly a reaction to the autocratic way Richard Nixon ran his White House. The adage for new presidents to recall is do not fight the last war.

The cabinet as an organizing principle around which to form an administration was done in by the inappropriate multiplication of cabinet departments. Presidents have been unable to resist the entreaties of special pleaders in this regard. Carter gave seats at the table to Education and Energy. Then, despite promises to abolish the two new departments, Reagan decided to keep them and to recommend Veterans for cabinet status. Individuals, too, were added on the basis of special claims, notably Office of Management and Budget Director Bert Lance (under Carter), CIA Director William Casey (under Reagan), and Environmental Protection Agency Administrator Carol Browner (under Clinton). The full cabinet became a crowd, not an advisory body.

Personnel problems also compromised the cabinet as an effective policymaking instrument. Carter lost respect for some members of his own cabinet, which resulted in the mass firing of July 1979. Reagan put in his cabinet some persons who lost the respect of important constituencies, notably James Watt at Interior.

The point is that a president must figure out what a cabinet can and ought to do, what a staff can and ought to do. Although it was hardly noticed by public and press, Reagan created what his aide Martin Anderson calls "a fairly elegant solution to the problem of how to effectively use cabinet members in the development of national policy." Reagan's cabinet council system consisted of six subgroups of cabinet members arrayed by topic, such as natural resources and the environment, commerce and trade, and so forth. In his book *Revolution*, Anderson reported that by the first week in December 1981 there had been 112 cabinet council meetings, roughly one-fifth of them chaired by the president. Anderson notes that on each of these occasions six or so cabinet officers and White House staff members talked before and after each meeting. "These short impromptu discussions among and between the president's policy advisers," he writes, "were probably as important to the advancement and development of his policy as the meetings themselves. Valuable pieces of information were exchanged, disagreements worked out privately, and Reagan's advisers got to know each other personally, intimately. It created, for a while, an unusual degree of harmony between two normally antagonistic groups, the White House staff and the cabinet."

Anderson's account of life within the Reagan White House may claim too much for what can be developed through cabinet councils. The system works best on matters of lesser importance to a president—natural gas deregulation, telecommunications regulation, federal credit policy, migrant worker health, all mentioned by Anderson as having been studied. But while less crucial than war or peace, boom or bust, presidential policies toward them are still important and may escape presidential attention unless some high-level mechanism such as a cabinet council is in place to force decisions. The White House should keep in touch with the cabinet for other reasons too—egomassaging, cheerleading, good communications, early warning. But if only as a strategy for secondary policy development, Reagan's cabinet council design deserves respectful consideration.

The sort of presidential actions that are given the "gate" suffix are often the fault of a president's judgment, not his advisory system. In the major scandal of the Reagan administration, when the president chose to sell arms to Iran, he was disregarding the advice of his secretaries of state and defense. Questions of legality aside, when Oliver North arranged to divert funds from the arms sale to the Nicaraguan contras, he violated rules of behavior that for four decades have restricted NSC staffs to an advisory role. Some "gates" are not susceptible to quick-fix organizational solutions. The report of the congressional investigating committees rightly concluded that "Congress cannot legislate good judgment."

An irony of the Iran-contra affair is that Reagan initially wanted to downgrade the importance of the National Security Council. His press spokesman Larry Speakes said "the President and his top aides . . . had such low regard for the position of NSC director that they paid little attention to those who held the post." If so, the president paid dearly for his indifference. (Ultimately, veteran public administrator Frank Carlucci was brought in to clean up the mess.)

The special review board, known as the Tower commission, that was created because of Iran-contra offered some sensible advice on the role of NSC directors. They should have direct access to the president and not have to report through some other White House official. They should not try to compete with the secretary of state and the secretary of defense as the "articulator of public policy." They should focus on "advice and management, not implementation and execution." The commission also gave a sound explanation of why the head of the NSC should not have to be confirmed by the Senate.

On every president's staff, deliberately or inadvertently, initially or eventually, there is a first among equals, a *primus inter pares*. The PIP will have different titles in different administrations—the assistant to the president, chief of staff, special counsel. And although the PIP is often thought of as a single person—a Sherman Adams under Eisenhower or John Sununu under Bush or Leon Panetta under Clinton—Richard Neustadt reminds us that there is almost always more than one "senior among seniors" in the White House. PIP is the acronym of a collective noun. The troika of James Baker, Edwin Meese, and Michael Deaver in Reagan's first term was a PIP.

The hierarchical model of a White House staff, usually drawn as a pyramid, is associated with Republicans Eisenhower and Nixon; the so-called spokes-in-a-wheel model, with the president at the epicenter, is associated with Democrats Roosevelt, Kennedy, and Johnson. Whatever genetic material makes one a Republican or a Democrat may well predispose a president to an organizational tendency. (Some organization theories are based on less evidence.) In fact, the more that is known about presidencies, the less the actual operation of the White House corresponds to boxes on a chart. Reagan's first-term White House, for instance, has been described as a hybrid of the spokes-in-a-wheel and chief-of-staff designs. And even Eisenhower's White House, which was considered the purest of pyramids, was considerably more spokish (or wheelish) than the textbook presentation.

The schema of political scientists, although pedagogically useful, do not truly reflect the world within the White House, where presidents tend to end up with a design that most resembles an isosceles trapezoid, a pyramid with its top chopped off. Presidents Ford and Carter ultimately relied on a semi-hierarchical staff system, a chain of command that permitted a small group of top aides direct access to the Oval Office.

The skills of a campaign manager are not what the new president most needs when picking the PIP, although not all campaign managers lack PIP skills. Such skills are more likely to be found in the campaigns of "insider" candidates. Hamilton Jordan, the architect of Carter's 1976 victory, claimed to be uninterested in the ways of Washington. Had Jordan been more interested, Carter might have had an easier time of it. Although on-the-job training is possible, it is hardly the most efficient way to get off to a fast start, especially since there is no shortage of those possessing the necessary skills. Reagan, another outsider, chose James Baker, a former official in the Ford administration, as his chief of staff, which then gave him the luxury of adding two California associates without Washington experience to complete a three-person PIP.

The PIP should be deeply schooled in and sensitive to the arcane ways of Washington. The PIP is the president's fail-safe mechanism, the last redoubt between him and a misstep. If the PIP does not know the location of all the traps that are set for a president in the capital, the president is likely to fall into one. This part of the job description is the pit of the PIP; the rest, public relations skills or policy development skills, can be brought into the White House in subordinate positions. PIPs who interpreted their responsibilities to the president largely in managerial terms—H. R. Haldeman in Nixon's administration or Donald Regan of Reagan's second term—served their presidents least well, but that need not have been their history had they also had the political antennae that the job requires. The PIP as manager, however, attracts enemies and thus should be expected to have a shortened lifespan in the job.

Changing PIPs in midstream—as Reagan did in 1985—is a perfectly sound strategy. Those at the top burn out. One can be a president's lightning rod for only so long. Replacing Baker-Meese-Deaver with Treasury Secretary Regan may have been considered inside the White House as the logical reflection of the differing needs of a first- and second-term presidency, but that Reagan should have swapped such a successful PIP for one that proved so unsuccessful also suggests that the qualities needed in the job had not been correctly assessed.

What background offers the greatest possibility for success? Former Senator Howard Baker, whose entire Washington career had been in Congress, is unique in that he was pressed into service to add his own prestige to a battered presidency. Other PIPs served in Congress for briefer periods (Sherman Adams and Donald Rumsfeld) or had been congressional staffers (Theodore Sorensen, Walter Jenkins, Richard Cheney). An understanding of the legislature is helpful, but ignorance of Congress is fatal.

Chief executives must be sorely tempted to turn their most trusted political friends into their PIP. After all, presidents are surrounded by strangers, supplicants, and sycophants. (Presidents need a friend, a role sometimes played by the First Spouse or by a court jester such as Dave Powers in the Kennedy White House.) Yet presidential friends who have become PIPs often have been the least effective. Bill Clinton's choice of boyhood buddy Thomas (Mack) McLarty as chief of staff was a high-wire appointment. Clinton's second PIP, Leon Panetta, a former California congressman, had the more traditional background of Washington insider.

While organizational design—or lack thereof—helps or hinders a president in reaching his goals, the decisive element in forming a successful administration is personnel selection. People. When the history of PIPs is written, it will illustrate the variety of ways that they have failed, personally and professionally. As Bruce Buchanan has put it, "Great chiefs of staff . . . may be no less difficult to locate than great presidents."

A long-standing tenet of public administration holds that the president's immediate staff should be small. "A large staff of personal assistants will reduce the president's ability to control those persons who speak directly in his name," according to a 1980 report of the National Academy of Public Administration. In 1988 Bradley Patterson estimated the number of people considered White House staffers: White House office (including Office of Policy Development), 568; National Security Council staff, 190; Office of the Vice President, 98; and 45 percent of the Office of Administration that directly supports the White House, 91. Total, 947.

Cuts in White House personnel can be negotiated with Congress on a reciprocal basis, since Congress is also under attack for the growth in its staff. Such negotiations, Samuel Popkin observes, "might approach the complexity of discussions on arms limitations with Russia." But the issue is really one of functions, not numbers.

The White House unit whose function is most often questioned is the Office of Public Liaison. Set up by Charles Colson in the Nixon administration, it has through the years amassed a body of presidential assistants to look after the concerns of business, labor, women, blacks, Hispanics, Jews, youth, the aged, Native Americans, consumers, ethnic groups, and farmers. Robert F. Bonitati, who served in the office in the Reagan White House, stated its problems succinctly: "1) It raises the visibility of many issues that do not deserve such attention; 2) it brings issues into the White House that should be settled elsewhere in the government; 3) it enhances the importance of the 'interest groups' being represented; and 4) it raises some troublesome questions about interest groups' advocates participating in policymaking decisions impacting their constituencies."

These White House aides thus represent the president to groups whose support he needs to govern and to get reelected, but they are more accurately described as presidential employees who represent certain interests within the White House. President Carter's experience with his counselor on aging, Nelson Cruikshank, makes this point. Joseph Califano, who was then secretary of Health, Education and Welfare, recounted this incident:

> On January 24th [1979], Carter called. "Cruikshank is threatening to resign as my Counselor on Aging unless he can speak out publicly against the Social Security reduction proposals."
>
> "I don't see how you can run your government and let a presidential aide attack the President's proposals," I responded.
>
> "Hamilton [Jordan] is concerned that if Cruikshank quits, he will organize all the senior citizens groups against us," Carter said.
>
> "Can't he just stay on and keep quiet? Just not support the proposals actively?" I suggested, seeking to salvage the situation.
>
> "I tried that. But Cruikshank wants to oppose them publicly," Carter said.

Cruikshank stayed on, and, in Califano's words, "delivered a stinging attack on the Social Security proposals before the [House] Committee on Aging." Special group advocacy within the White House increased under Reagan.

Most former aides who have commented on White House management suggest trimming its size. "As with the ships of the Spanish Armada, size is a crippling handicap, not a source of strength," wrote Carter administration officials Ben W. Heineman, Jr., and Curtis A. Hessler. Mitchell E. Daniels, Jr., who was Reagan's assistant for political affairs from 1985 to 1987, proposed abolishing the White House political office, preferring to connect the president to his party by putting the national chairman in the cabinet. More appropriate, in my opinion, would be to give the party chairman the additional title of assistant to the president and transfer the duties of the political office to the national committee, which would breathe new life into the party system and leverage the president's political outreach all at the same time.

There is one area, however, where presidential assistants argue that White House growth is justified. "[The Office of] Legislative Affairs can no longer just deal with Congressional leadership on a particular item," commented Franklin L. Lavin of the Reagan staff.

"Important votes, such as the Bork nomination [to the Supreme Court] or contra aid, involve 'hand-to-hand combat'—working with any number of Members to get their votes. This means Legislative Affairs must be a larger organization." A White House office could be designed to parallel the congressional whip system, composed of presidential assistants each responsible for the care and feeding of legislators from a certain geographic area. Unfortunately, the probable result is that legislators' demands on the president would increase faster than the president could add lobbyists.

While the White House organization and its size will not remain static—it will respond to political, technological, and institutional changes—a new president would do well to start from the premise that small is still beautiful.

As he was about to take office, John Kennedy is supposed to have said to a friend, "I must make the appointments now. A year hence I will know who I really want to appoint." The implication is that a year hence he would also know whom he wanted to fire. It is not frivolous for a president to want to remove an able appointee whose only crime is that he makes the president feel uncomfortable, as was the case when Gerald Ford fired Defense Secretary James Schlesinger. A president, like the rest of us, usually has to believe that people are congenial in order to rely on them. Yet presidents are notoriously bad at dismissing people. The inability to fire is almost a presidential trait. It is not because presidents are uniquely kindhearted. Nor is it merely that they hate to admit mistakes. Nor even that they usually have had limited experience at firing people. It is because most people who become presidents have spent much of their lives seeking office, an activity in which not making enemies is important. More than calculation is involved. Like Willie Loman in *Death of a Salesman*, politicians want to be more than liked, they want to be well liked. Sometimes a president will devise ways to work around a cabinet officer who displeases him. Franklin Roosevelt, for instance, chose to deal with the War Department through the assistant secretary when Harry Woodring was his Pentagon chief. This is a dangerous design, which ultimately only compounds a president's problems. The question, then, is how to get rid of unwanted appointees and remain popular. Indeed, the success of an administration can rest on finding the answer.

In some cases there is no answer. There was no way that Nixon could have gracefully removed Watergate prosecutor Archibald Cox. And occasionally the opposite situation occurs: a president may want to call attention to a dismissal, either because a dereliction of public trust is involved or as a warning to other appointees. In effect, the president is saying he will not tolerate certain kinds of behavior.

Most of the time, however, a president simply wants an unwanted appointee to go away without making a fuss. That happens more often than is usually noted. Every new administration has some members who ultimately realize that coming to Washington was a mistake and quietly take leave of the place. But what is the best way to get rid of those appointees who are highly visible, have their own constituencies, contacts in the press corps, the potential to make trouble, and do not want to leave? *Offer them another job.* From the president's vantage point, it is the former official, the insider who becomes the outsider, who could be dangerous. Assume that the unwanted official is not untalented, merely in the wrong place. Finding the right place involves the fine art of equivalency, balancing the prestige of two positions—head of a domestic cabinet-level agency and a judgeship at the U.S. Court of Appeals level, for example.

Lyndon Johnson was the grand master at playing equivalency. For example, he respected Robert McNamara, although he was discomforted by his defense secretary's closeness to the Kennedys. By 1967 McNamara was uneasy with the president's Vietnam policy. As the presidential election year approached, Johnson surely was calculating the damage the Pentagon chief could cause if he resigned and made his objections to the war public, especially if Robert Kennedy decided to challenge the president for the Democratic nomination. So McNamara was offered and accepted the presidency of the World Bank. Not only had a potentially troubling political problem been finessed, but the World Bank had been placed in capable hands. Of two others who left the Johnson cabinet for positions of relative equivalency, Health, Education, and Welfare Secretary Anthony Celebrezze, a former mayor of Cleveland, was made a federal judge, and Postmaster General John Gronouski, the first Polish-American to be in a president's cabinet, was appointed ambassador to Poland. (There is an added plus if the new job is out of Washington.)

Not all presidents, however, have played the equivalency game with such skill. Kennedy, in wanting to remove Chester Bowles as under secretary of state, and Nixon, in wanting to remove Robert Finch as HEW secretary, could not devise the appropriate equivalencies and ended up giving them nebulous White House assignments that fooled no one.

The difficulty that Donald Regan had in removing Margaret Heckler as secretary of Health and Human Services attests to the heavy-handedness of President Reagan's chief of staff. But the inability to get rid of Regan in a neat and expeditious fashion was a near-fatal blow to that presidency. Had an equivalency been worked out, such as making Regan the ambassador extraordinary and plenipotentiary to the Court of St. James—a title likely to soothe a bruised ego—he would not have published his destructive account of life within the White House while Reagan was still in office. It is an object lesson in knowing when and how to fire unwanted officials.

Finally, to ease his policy process, a president must learn to deal with leaks. Leaking, as defined in Washington, is the unauthorized giving of information to a journalist. The rules of the game are that the journalist must not identify the leaker and that the information must be sufficiently newsworthy that someone in government would not wish to have it publicly known at that time. Leaking has a long, and sometimes distinguished, history. Elie Abel suggests that the first significant leak exposed a secret U.S. arms transaction with France. The year was 1778 and the leaker was Tom Paine.

Leaks, said President Ford, are a "real pain." They produce embarrassing news stories, throw off a president's timing, and consume an inordinate amount of high-level attention within the White House. If they get out of hand, they can lead to bad presidential management practices. With the threat of a leak hanging over his head like Damocles' sword, the president and his White House aides may unreasonably hurry a decision, or severely limit the number of advisers who should be consulted, or keep out technical experts who are not considered political loyalists. Donald Regan even claims that the "root of the [Iran-contra] scandal may well lie in the fact that [NSC heads Robert] McFarlane and [John] Poindexter and their assistants were, in a sense, driven mad by leaks." In short, the price paid for preventing leaks may far exceed the damage caused by unauthorized publication.

Ignoring leaks assumes, of course, that they are not important national security secrets. Government has a right to have secrets. Could the United States have reestablished relations with China if Henry Kissinger could not have carried on secret discussions with the Chinese? Doubtful. Advocates of free speech should not be cavalier about such concerns. Still, very few serious leaks have occurred, partly because the American press practices self-censorship in such cases, and more often because the government is very good at keeping secret its real secrets.

President Reagan complained that leaks "reached a new high" in his administration. Some have argued that so many leaks occurred because Reagan brought into government so many ideologues willing to fight their battles through the media. If that argument is correct, then the solution for future presidents is to choose staff of more temperate mien. But a Harvard study, published in 1986, found little correlation between leaking and ideology. The Reagan administration reached a record for leaks because leaking has become such a routine and accepted part of Washington behavior and because as government gets more complex, more documents will be needed to produce decisions, more copying machines will be available to reproduce documents, and more reporters will be available to receive the documents.

So what advice might be useful to a new president? First, he should understand who is apt to be a leaker. Reagan's initial impulse was to blame bureaucrats. But it is a rare bureaucrat who engages in leaking. The civil servants' world faces inward. They know how to work within their own agency to thwart a president. Besides, most journalists are outside the bureaucrats' ken and represent risk beyond possible gain. Presidents also tend to blame leaks on their press officers. But the press office tries to avoid a practice that antagonizes the reporters who do not receive the leaks. The leakers, a president must be told, are his own political appointees.

Second, once the president understands who the leakers are, he can more readily accept the next proposition: a president is more leaked for than leaked against. That may not seem to be the case when he reads his morning paper, but it is true in a four- or eight-year balance sheet. When the president's side does the leaking, however, a leak is not a leak; it is a plant.

Third, as President Carter said, there is no "effective way to deal with the situation." Attempts to stop leakers, which usually involve wiretaps and lie detectors, are always painful, possibly illegal, rarely successful, and inevitably get a bad press.

The appropriate posture for a president is to make a clear distinction between leaking and espionage. The latter is illegal and cannot be tolerated. Keep the classification of documents within reasonable bounds; do not tempt journalists by stamping SECRET unless the purpose is to get something in the press. Be prepared to make a case with editors for not publishing classified documents that they have acquired. Use cabinet and staff meetings to remind high-level appointees of their obligations in this regard. Consider personality as a factor in making top appointments (Secretary of State Alexander Haig and NSC Adviser Richard Allen were a twosome destined to produce leaks). Above all, have fortitude. As Henry Kissinger said after he left government, "You see, most of the leaks—if you are philosophical about it—go away. I mean, they're unpleasant, but so what? If you ignore them, most of them are not of that huge significance."

To be most useful, advice to a president-elect should fit a set of circumstances. Each election produces its own dynamic and helps shape what a president wishes to accomplish and what is politically feasible. Does the president win a narrow victory, similar to the contests of 1960 and 1968? Does he win in a landslide, as in 1932 and 1952? Does his party win control of both houses of Congress? Of one house? Of no houses? In the course of the campaign, the president-elect incurs debts and obligations—to people, to groups, to policies. But there is one piece of advice to all presidents that is guaranteed: Prepare to be surprised.

# The President
# and the Press

Although nineteenth-century presidents submitted themselves to occasional private interviews with friendly journalists, the White House was not a regular beat for Washington reporters until 1896, when William Price, of the *Washington Star*, stationed himself outside the presidential mansion to interview Grover Cleveland's visitors. Price's initiative inspired imitators, and, on a winter day in 1902, Theodore Roosevelt saw reporters huddled around the north portico and invited them inside. Later that year he had a pressroom built in the new west wing, which, historian George Juergens has noted, "conferred a sort of legitimacy on their presence. . . . They were no longer there as guests of the president."

Woodrow Wilson was the first chief executive to hold regular press conferences, initiated when 125 reporters crowded into the East Room on Saturday afternoon, March 15, 1913, eleven days after Wilson's inauguration. Joseph Tumulty, the president's secretary, also gave a daily briefing for the White House regulars, about 30 reporters from the major news organizations, just as presidential secretary William Loeb had done during Roosevelt's administration.

From *Encyclopedia of the American Presidency*, vols. 3 and 4 (Simon and Schuster, 1994); and *Critical Choices* (Brookings, 1989).

Roosevelt and Wilson, unlike William Howard Taft, whose term fell between theirs, appreciated the importance of news to presidential leadership. And if activist presidents had uses for the press, so too did the expansionist newspaper and magazine industry want energetic White House occupants who could help it sell its products.

Future presidents might have learned from the ways Roosevelt and Wilson manipulated the press by taking advantage of the conventions and necessities of news gathering or simply by intimidating reporters. Roosevelt was the inventor of colorful phrases ("malefactors of great wealth," "bully pulpit," "my hat's in the ring"), precursors of the sound bites of the television age. He was an expert at releasing information to gain maximum attention, sometimes putting out a story on Sunday night that would gain extra coverage on Monday morning, an otherwise slow time for news. He mastered the trial balloon, a technique designed to measure support for a proposal without his actually endorsing it. He used calculated leaks of previously secret information, sometimes to undercut an opponent. And he was known to restrict the access of reporters who had offended him.

Wilson eventually stopped holding press conferences, citing national security concerns as his excuse, but Warren G. Harding, the only newspaper editor ever to have been elected president, reinstituted them, insisting, however, that reporters' questions be submitted in advance in writing. He also invented the term *White House spokesman* to allow him to speak without direct attribution. Calvin Coolidge and Herbert Hoover continued the written-question rule. Twice-a-week press conferences thus became institutionalized in the 1920s on terms very advantageous to presidents.

During most of the twentieth century the history of presidential press relations has been largely a history of the press conference. At one time the *New York Times* even hired a limousine to get its reporters back to the office, since, according to bureau chief James Reston, "Many of these conferences took place near deadline, when it was hard to find a taxi." Franklin Roosevelt held 998 press conferences (and one private interview) during his twelve-plus years in office, and, although oral questioning was permitted, most of his answers had to be used without quoting him or used on background (meaning without White House attribution) or were off the record (meaning not for publication).

If, as is often assumed, the presidency and the press are adversari-
ally balanced, on a sort of symbolic teeter-totter, the presidency was
on the upswing through the administration of Franklin Roosevelt,
but it started to come down when Harry S Truman took office.
Responding to the growth of the press corps, Truman moved the
sessions—reduced to one a week—out of the Oval Office, an
intimate setting, and into an auditorium, called the Indian Treaty
Room, across the street from the White House. The new format,
according to communications expert Carolyn Smith, changed the
atmosphere "from conversation to competitive questioning." Moreover, wrote the political scientist Elmer Cornwell, "While F.D.R.
was so conspicuously in charge of the conference at all times, Mr.
Truman was either disinclined or unable to exert similar control."
By the end of the Truman presidency the conferences were being
recorded and portions released for use on radio. Eisenhower, the
next president, had his conferences filmed for delayed broadcast on
television; Kennedy inaugurated live TV conferences.

Putting reporters into the picture did not necessarily make them
more assertive; it did, however, offer that potential, which was
sometimes realized by television journalists on their way to celebrity.
In an often-noted exchange in March 1974 Nixon asked CBS
correspondent Dan Rather, "Are you running for something?"
Rather replied, "No sir, Mr. President, are you?" Newspaper reporters, at the same time, were being given new freedom (perhaps
because of TV competition) to go beyond the "objective" style of
wire-service stories to interpretation of a president's performance.

There were various means by which presidents might counter
what they increasingly viewed as a less-than-friendly White House
press corps. One way was to hold fewer press conferences. Although
Eisenhower met the press twice a month, Nixon's press conferences
averaged one every other month. Another way was to hold conferences with reporters in other regions of the country, who—according to the conventional wisdom of Washington—would be less
challenging. A third way, perfected by Reagan's adviser Michael
Deaver, was to lure TV cameras with situations and pictures so
compelling that they assured favorable coverage (for example, the
scene of the president at a Normandy beach on the fortieth anniver-
sary of D-day).

A fourth way to counter the White House press corps was to solicit expert advice and to hire more staff in addition to the White House press secretary and his office. Eisenhower sought the counsel of actor-director Robert Montgomery when preparing for TV appearances. Nixon created the Office of Communications, originally to coordinate governmentwide information efforts. Assistants were assigned to help journalists outside the Washington beltway. When presidents were candidates for reelection, other resources were available. As Jeb Magruder, who was deputy director of Nixon's communications office, recalled, "We were seeking not only to speak through the media in the usual fashion—press releases, news conferences—but to speak around the media, much of which we considered hostile, to take our message directly to the people." By the time of the Reagan presidency, according to Gary R. Orren of Harvard University, approximately 25 percent of the White House senior staff were employed in public relations jobs.

While the press conference has been called a critically important means of communication, it seldom makes important news. If a president has something important to say, he can and does find far better vehicles than press conferences. The press conference, however, could be said to make important news if a president seriously misspeaks (which has happened only once, under Truman, when he implied that the atomic bomb might be used against China during the Korean War), or if reporters, by their clever questioning, get the president to reveal information that he would have wanted to keep to himself. But any politician who has reached the rank of president knows how to duck, bob, and weave sufficiently to stay out of trouble.

Columnist William Rusher views press conferences as "metaphorical bullfights. . . . The president is the bull. The excitement stems from the tension over which of the major protagonists will triumph—the bull or the matador." Still, as George Reedy, one of Lyndon Johnson's press secretaries, has pointed out, "The President has the advantage since he can make a quip, evade the question, decline to answer on grounds of national security or simply turn to another reporter. It's his news conference, not the media's." A president also can control the conference with an opening statement, by scripting answers to the expected questions, and even by planting questions with friendly reporters.

Nevertheless, sensible people are convinced that press conferences are high-stake gambles for a president. Questions often sound tough. Questioners often sound confrontational. Press conferences are also viewed as serious contests because reporters are constantly telling us that that is what they are—an impression that is good for business and for their egos. Yet when one reads the transcript of a press conference, what is asked and how easily it is parried produce a different reality. A president, of course, also has a vested interest in perpetuating the notion that answering reporters' questions is a dangerous business.

More frequent presidential press conferences would downplay the role of the press secretary's daily briefing, which is to be fervently desired. The typical White House noon briefing has come to resemble an unruly fraternity party, where very little news of any value is produced. If the reporters' next meeting with the president would never be more than thirteen days away, the press secretary's all-purpose reply could be "ask the president."

As the White House staff grows larger, it also grows more specialized. Presidential assistants, beyond the core of aides who directly advise the president, are increasingly economists, scientists, and other professional specialists. The White House press corps has also grown in size, but it is not any more specialized. It is a general assignment beat writ large. Many reporters get their White House assignment as a reward for covering the winning candidate during the campaign. News organizations use the change of presidents as an excuse to rotate reporters, creating mobility within otherwise turgid personnel systems. (The wire services, which tend to treat the White House as a permanent assignment, are exceptions.)

The rationale is that campaign reporters make valuable contacts with the people who will become White House assistants—a dubious proposition because in Washington journalism who you work for is more important than who you know. A practice of short tenures also works to ensure that White House reporters lack institutional memory. Moreover, these reporters are seldom experts in the substance of White House news; they are not specialists in foreign policy or economics or many of the other subjects that White House policy covers.

A president can always push news away from the White House press corps. The Treasury Department, rather than the White House, could announce major economic developments, for example. Reporters on that beat are better equipped to deal with financially complex matters. And specialized reportage has become noticeably more knowledgeable in recent years, which suggests that an administration could receive more serious coverage if it altered the release points of the information over which it has control. For most presidents, though, the thought of separating themselves from publicity is cruel and unusual punishment.

Because it is not within a president's power to reorganize the Washington news-gathering system or reassign reporters (although some have tried, including a Nixonian effort to be rid of Dan Rather), the next best hope is to seek to educate the White House press corps. The president's science adviser might conduct weekly briefings on scientific matters that affect federal policy, the Council of Economic Advisers could do the same for macroeconomic effects of policy, and the Office of Management and Budget could conduct sessions on the intricacies of the budget process, just as it has done in the past for incoming White House staffs. This suggestion would, however, require an additional criterion in the job descriptions of presidential advisers: the president's experts would have to be able to explain their expertise to the reporters whose job it is to explain the president's policies to their listeners and readers.

The first White House aide to have press relations as his sole responsibility—the equivalent of being press secretary to the president—was George Akerson, who served (not very successfully) from 1929 to 1931 under Herbert Hoover. But the role of the press secretary came of age during the administration of Franklin D. Roosevelt when Stephen Early ran the press office. Although new communications technologies and the growth of the White House press corps have engendered changes in the office, the press secretary's basic functions have remained relatively constant. Press secretaries still conduct daily briefings for reporters on the White House beat, help the president prepare for press conferences, handle press arrangements for presidential trips and vacations, respond to requests from individual reporters for interviews and information, and put out press releases and the texts of presidential speeches and messages.

Strictly speaking, the press secretary is not a policy adviser, although the law of propinquity—the power that can emanate from being close to the powerful—has from time to time affected staffers who have occupied the slot. For example, Bill Moyers, press secretary to Lyndon Johnson, was one of six officials composing what was known as the Tuesday Cabinet, which held weekly Vietnam War decisionmaking sessions.

The press secretary's domain largely involves handling Washington-based reporters, with other media relations taken care of by other White House offices. The press office staff had grown to seventeen by 1991, with three deputy press secretaries, one of whom was in charge of foreign policy issues and also served as the spokesperson for the national security adviser. Junior staff, responsible for turning out press releases, are housed in what is called the lower press office, which is adjacent to the White House briefing room. (During Richard Nixon's first term the White House swimming pool, located between the president's residence and his office in the west wing, was decked over to create this working area for reporters.)

There were eighteen presidential press secretaries from Akerson through Marlin Fitzwater, who served under Ronald Reagan and George Bush. All were white males, usually of early middle years. (Dee Dee Myers, Bill Clinton's press secretary, was thirty-two when she became the first female press secretary in 1993.) The average age at time of appointment was forty-two; the youngest, Ronald Ziegler, who served under Nixon, was thirty; the oldest, Charles Ross, sixty, died in office during the Truman presidency. Half had served as Washington correspondents. Six, including Clinton's second press secretary, Michael McCurry, had never been journalists. Those whose entire careers had been in journalism were among the least successful press secretaries; the most successful were either very close to the presidents they served regardless of their previous occupations or had had experience in public affairs or political press relations.

Perhaps the most successful was James Hagerty, who served under Dwight Eisenhower. Hagerty had been a *New York Times* reporter, press secretary to a governor of New York, and spokesman for the

1952 Republican presidential campaign. Hagerty is credited with creating new standards for frankness when Eisenhower suffered a heart attack in 1955. For three weeks he held five briefings a day, releasing such intimate details as the number of bowel movements recorded on the president's medical chart. (At the other extreme, press secretaries do not always offer the whole truth; for example, Reagan's press secretary Larry Speakes said that an invasion of Grenada was "preposterous" on the day before the United States invaded that island in 1983.)

At Hagerty's first meeting with White House reporters in 1953, he told them, "When I say to you, 'I don't know,' I mean I don't know. When I say, 'No comment,' it means I'm not talking, but not necessarily any more than that. Aside from that, I'm here to help you get the news. I am also here to work for one man, who happens to be the president. And I will do that to the best of my ability." Being between president and press creates what Walter Wurfel, a deputy press secretary under President Carter, has called "the fundamental duality to the role of the White House press secretary." Wurfel wrote that the press secretary is "a government official paid by the taxpayers and is responsible for supplying information to the public. On the other hand, he is a political appointee answerable only to the president, and the president views the spokesman's job to be that of putting the most favorable light on his administration." Some of the press secretaries who came directly from journalism were the most affected by this fundamental duality. Jerald terHorst, who left the Washington bureau of the *Detroit News* to become Gerald Ford's first press secretary, lasted only thirty days, resigning when he could not support Ford's decision to pardon former President Nixon.

Thirty-nine White House reporters, interviewed in the summer of 1991 about their preferences among the press secretaries they had known, often mentioned desirable personal and professional qualities. Among the personal qualities they appreciated were friendliness, an unwillingness to embarrass reporters, a sense of humor, and honesty. Professional qualities they admired included an understanding of journalists' needs, a lack of favoritism, and good briefing skills. But overwhelmingly what they wanted in a White House press secretary was confidence that what he told them came from an intimate and immediate knowledge of what the president was thinking. They appreciated, for example, the almost father–son relationship between Carter and press secretary Jody Powell. Reporters also enjoyed Pierre Salinger's company, but they knew that Kennedy had kept him in the dark about the Bay of Pigs invasion, and they respected George Reedy's intelligence, but they knew that Johnson withheld information from him. Ultimately, then, as George Christian, another of Johnson's press secretaries, once said, press secretaries' "style will be shaped by the presidents they work for, or they won't be there long."

Press relations between a president and the journalists who report from the White House are often described as if they are static. For those who see the interaction between president and press primarily as a political tug-of-war, the media represent either a liberal or a conservative challenge to the president. Those who attack the press from the right cite evidence, mostly in the form of straw polls, showing that reporters are overwhelmingly in favor of liberal presidents, presidential policies, and presidential candidates. Those who accuse the press of a conservative bias cite evidence that publishers are overwhelmingly in favor of more conservative presidents, policies, and candidates.

A description that better reflects the fluidity of the relationship, however, has been created by Michael Baruch Grossman and Martha Joynt Kumar, among others. Their scheme shows that interaction between the president and the press goes through three phases during an administration, which Grossman and Kumar call *alliance, competition,* and *detachment.* In their judgment,

> There is a period at the beginning of an administration when the White House and news organizations appear to be allies in producing and disseminating news. This is followed by clashes over news and information so great that the two sides appear to be adversaries. In a third stage the intensity of the competition burns out and is replaced by a relationship that is more structured and less intense than that in either of the first two periods.

The start of a presidency is a time of fermentation. New people and new ideas arrive in Washington, and, from a reporter's point of view, this is a time for good stories. From the president's vantage point, these stories tend to be favorable. Then the administration has its first foreign crisis or its first domestic scandal, weaknesses in personnel and organization begin to appear, and the novelty of new personalities wears off. These things make for good stories for reporters, but the stories are no longer favorable to the president. Ultimately, president and press, having mutual needs, learn to live with each other like an old married couple who can no longer surprise one another. Finally, reporters begin to look forward to the next president, when the process will start again. Thus the objective of the press to get good stories and the objective of the president to get favorable attention sometimes coincide, sometimes not.

# Toward a
# More
# Functional
# Presidency

The history of the modern presidency has been one of growing presidential involvement in management. Much of the growth in the White House staff has been caused by presidents' attempts to take over the operation of high-priority programs (poverty and drug abuse, for example) or to exercise greater oversight, and eventually control, over the bureaucracy. It is hardly accidental that the Bureau of the Budget was renamed the Office of Management and Budget. All major studies since the Brownlow committee report of 1937 have recommended giving presidents additional tools for management as a means of increasing their control over the executive branch. But one result of making presidents managers is that they spend more and more time doing what they do badly and presumably less time doing what only presidents can handle.

There are various ways out of this dilemma. One solution would be to elect managers to the presidency. If, in fact, the responsibilities of a president are largely managerial, this step would be logical and would only await proper recognition on the part of the electorate. Yet such a view represents a profound misunderstanding: the main presidential role is to make choices that are ultimately political. The

From *Organizing the Presidency*, rev. ed. (Brookings, 1988).

president is the nation's chief political officer. He tries to control a process that is quintessentially political, and the political process primarily concerns distribution not production. It decides who gets how much of what is available, not how to make more available at less cost. A political process cannot be managed in the sense that a corporation is managed, for political decisions are judged according to their fairness, both in the way they are made and in their perceived effect.

Assuming that the bigger the federal government, the more unmanageable it becomes, a second way of relieving presidents of superfluous tasks would be for the government to do less, or to turn over more of its revenues to states and localities to do things that Americans expect government to do or to contract with private parties to perform services that it has previously delivered. The proposition then becomes: if the president cannot satisfactorily manage the federal establishment, find ways to decrease what must be managed rather than to increase the managerial ability of the president. These are political decisions, of course. They could be made if the electorate strongly indicated a desire to move in these directions. The electorate's choice would, however, still leave many activities for the federal government to manage.

A third solution would be to reorganize the executive branch to reflect a more realistic approach to solving problems and delivering services. Most departments represent a collection of past answers to yesterday's most important problems, or past demands on elected officials by important special-interest groups, and of long-forgotten bureaucratic fights over jurisdiction. Given the difficulty of changing existing arrangements, presidents have continued to create new agencies and to pull new problems into the White House, where their authority is greater. The piecemeal history of recent reorganizations has been that of consolidating related activities, of putting all transportation matters in one department, all housing matters in another, and so on. But as housing and transportation, for example, have increasingly seemed interconnected, proposals have been made to create a Department of Community Development and similar functional groupings. Such suggestions would result in fewer and larger departments. From the president's standpoint, the advantage would be in reducing the number of officials he has to track. The "lesser" departments, which are apt to be overlooked by presidents, might be expected to be raised in stature and visibility by consolidation.

But while consolidation can equalize the departments' access to the president, the case has not been firmly made that consolidation could avoid creating bureaucratic monstrosities. If the problems of government are partly the result of bigness, are bigger departments the solution? The histories of the two giants of the federal bureaucracy—the Department of Health, Education and Welfare (before Education was made into a separate department) and the Department of Defense—suggest that there is such a thing as optimum size. Putting together several small agencies may produce greater efficiency; creating agencies that employ 100,000 people may produce greater inefficiency and further loss of presidential control. A lesson of the Pentagon reorganization is that presidents had greater control over spending when each military service had to compete before them than they now have when a consolidated department irons out its differences in private and presents the chief executive with a common front.

Whether agencies are big or small, however, organization along functional lines makes sense. Government becomes more understandable—no small consideration in a democratic society—and the prospects of jurisdictional disputes may be lessened. Moreover, functional divisions should increase agency accountability to the president and Congress.

Still, the question arises whether reorganizations can long remain in phase with changing priorities, crises, and fads: what might have been established in 1970 as a Department of Environment was ultimately created in 1977 as a Department of Energy. Government organizations constantly drift into dysfunctionality, and presidents rely on distorted ad hoc arrangements. Yet presidents must also be aware that there can be problems of excessive reorganization. "Who is going to be the new boss? Will she like me? What's the latest rumor?" Constant tinkering takes a toll in the administration of federal programs.

The best time to reorganize is as promptly as possible after a president assumes office (which, of course, is the time presidents are least qualified to act). Moreover, changes should be made in such a way that successive presidents can undo them. Whatever format is easiest to change, reverse, or abolish is best in the long run. Changes that can be made informally or by executive order are preferable to those that are formal and statutory, just as changes that can be made by statute are to be preferred to those that require constitutional amendment.

A fourth solution to the problem of management is for presidents to revert to a pre–New Deal level of power. Such proposals have come from Barbara Tuchman and others who, in the wake of Vietnam and Watergate, have feared presidents' initiatives more than they have been troubled by their failing to tame the lions of bureaucracy. The proposals of these scholars would ensure that federal agencies would continue to operate as independent forces, answerable to the president only when they needed his support, and that a 535-member legislature would assume a greater role in operational activities. But although life without a president may sometimes have a fantasylike attractiveness, no society as large and complex as the United States could proceed for long on the waning momentum of bureaucracy. Autonomous agencies are certainly preferable to presidential corruption; they are not, however, a substitute for enlightened presidential leadership. The American people elect presidents, not civil servants. The problem of how to ensure responsive and humane government performance is real and growing. The question is how can it be achieved within a democratic framework and within the capacities of the types of persons most likely to be elected president?

It is time to rethink the appropriate role of the president, to again define the basic functions that presidents perform (generally with the concurrence of Congress). These are presidential functions that require the active participation of the president:

—Devising policy to ensure the security of the country, with special attention to situations that could involve the nation in war.

—Devising a legislative program that presents recommendations for new initiatives, presumably ranking them in order of importance.

—Preparing the annual budget, which recommends changes in the size of existing programs.

—Sharing responsibility for adjustments of the economy engineered by the government.

—Selecting noncareer government personnel.

—Informing the people and their representatives in Congress of actions taken or proposed and presenting assessments of the state of the nation and of U.S. involvement around the world.

—Resolving conflicts between departments and seeking coordination of departmental policies.

—Overseeing the executive branch with some shared authority for promoting efficient and humane services and for ferreting out corruption.

This job description does not include the president's role as tone setter for the nation ("moral leader" strikes me as too grand for an elected politician). A president should be able to provide effective reassurances and exhortations in difficult periods, give a heightened sense of national purpose, and put before the citizenry a vision of a better society. But such abilities are most affected by the people's trust in a president based on his past record, personal conduct, rhetorical skills, factors such as being in office during a "just" war, and other matters that are not closely correlated with a president's methods of organizing his administration.

Nor does my list include the ceremonial functions of a president. Some have viewed these duties as frivolous, as a waste of valuable presidential time, and have suggested that they be turned over to the vice president or that a separate ceremonial head of state be created. (In fact, many of these duties are currently performed by the president's spouse and children.) But ceremonial duties, which can be adjusted to fit the time available, can be useful in keeping a president in touch with the people, in helping create a sense of national unity, and in endorsing worthwhile undertakings.

Much that goes on at the White House is done in the president's name—reports to Congress, greetings and routine letters, proclamations, appointments to honorific positions, and so forth. A book published in 1970 devotes 166 pages to listing just those activities that are a president's legal responsibilities, such as annexing any rock, island, or key not belonging to another government and on which a deposit of guano is found. But most of these duties do not require more of a president's time than the incessant signing of his name, which even under Truman occurred more than 400 times a day. The distinction between responsibilities that need a president's personal attention and those that do not is well illustrated by the experiences of government during the months before Nixon's resignation. The apparent paralysis of the presidency in fact affected few of the routine operations of government.

There are guideposts along the path to a more functional presidency. Keep presidents out of matters that are not presidential in nature. Remove the dangers of an overextended White House staff. Guide presidents in the direction of seeking advice from those who will be responsible for policy implementation. Improve the responsiveness of the bureaucracy to the wishes of the electorate by increasing the leverage of department officials whose fate depends on public mandate. Yet these alone are no guarantee that there will be no Vietnams, no Watergates, no Iran-contra affairs.

There can be no assurance that presidents will always act wisely, that they will always get good advice, or that they will accept good advice when it is offered. The history of Lyndon Johnson in Vietnam is that he received advice against escalating the war from a wide variety of sources. The history of Watergate argues that the cover-up, the act for which Richard Nixon was forced to resign, was a decision made by the president, not the product of a faulty system of advice. Watergate, of course, does reflect on the staff members who assisted Nixon in the cover-up, but in the end it is the president who sets the tone for his administration. The Reagan history is more confusing, less clear-cut: a first term in which he was given credit for having perfect pitch in orchestrating the performance of government and a second term of Iran-contra and a malfunctioning White House staff. Then there was a term of George Bush that produced great gains for America abroad and was tone-deaf at home.

Yet Bush's lethargic response to a troubled economy, Reagan's strange detachment from his own government, Carter's mechanical conception of leadership, Nixon's moral obtuseness, Johnson's misplaced machismo—all are useful reminders that organizational design, or lack thereof, may help or hinder a president in reaching his goals, but the decisive element of the presidency remains the mettle of the president.

# The Once and Future Presidency

The way that Americans regard their chief executive has changed remarkably since the first president was chosen unanimously by the electors in 1789. Although only George Washington was awarded this office without opposition, throughout most of the nation's history the American people would have agreed with British statesman John Bright, who said of the presidency in 1861, "To my mind there is nothing more worthy of reverence and obedience." After World War II, however, something strange happened: every president except one—Dwight D. Eisenhower—lost favor in the opinion polls the longer he remained in office. Even George Bush, whose popularity shot up for a shining moment after the 1991 Persian Gulf War, was defeated the next year. Of late, Americans clearly have not felt much reverence for their presidents.

Various explanations have been suggested for this deterioration of approval. Some say that the only problem with the presidency is that inferior people have been elected. "The country is filled with individuals with the potential of a Washington, Jefferson, Lincoln, Wilson, or FDR," declared historian Henry Steele Commager in a 1979 interview; "but where do these people go? Perhaps into

From *Every Four Years*, rev. ed. (Smithsonian Books, 1984).

science or the arts, certainly not into national politics." Recent presidents may have been less capable than their predecessors. Yet it is always tempting to romanticize the past, and we ought not forget that for every Washington there was a Zachary Taylor; for every Lincoln, at least one James Buchanan; and a Harding as well as a Wilson.

Still, it is probably true that the way our system of nominating major-party candidates has evolved does put a premium on those who are best able to raise huge sums of money and run helter-skelter through forty state primary elections—abilities that are not necessarily the ones most essential to performing the duties of chief executive. As a corrective, partial public financing of the presidential contest was tried for the first time in 1976, and some reformers have proposed holding a national primary. It is worth recalling, however, that a "bad" system, one characterized by political bosses making deals in smoke-filled back rooms, produced Lincoln and the Roosevelts.

Another explanation for the chronic slippage in popular esteem that has bedeviled recent presidents is based on the proposition that great leaders are produced in response to great crises. There are several apparent instances of this in American history, but most often cited is Lincoln's leadership during the Civil War and Franklin Roosevelt's in the Great Depression. Leadership may thus be a product of the times rather than of the availability and election of sterling candidates. It is also true, however, that in times of crisis the American people have generally rallied around the president, offering a form of popular support that may actually be a requisite for effective leadership. Furthermore, while the theory that great troubles somehow generate great leaders seems to have the ring of truth, it is little comfort to a nation whose present problems may not be cataclysmic, as in 1861 or 1933, yet are certainly serious enough to demand a very high order of leadership.

But there is yet another idea to consider, an idea epitomized in the words of Henry Steele Commager: "The President is increasingly a creature of society—a creature of its psychology, its standards, its expectations, a creature of its advertising. . . . We get the kind of men who are not bold, who are not innovative, who are not resourceful—or, even if they could be, they still won't risk it." What this amounts to saying is that, yes, the presidency is in a sorry state, but the fault lies in ourselves, not the White House. How does one respond? Certainly one may marshal evidence to counter the proposition that our boldness and resourcefulness have left us. We are a people, for example, who still produce billionaires in one generation in businesses as dissimilar as Microsoft and K-Mart and whose scientists still garner Nobel Prizes almost yearly. If our failures are evident in our leaders, then so too are our strengths. Each must assess for himself our strengths and weaknesses.

My own view of what has been happening to the presidency—without meaning to imply that the problems are subject to only one interpretation—is that it has become harder to run a democratic country. The so-called failure in leadership can be seen in other parts of the world and is reflected in a greater rate of government turnovers wherever free elections are held. In the United States the so-called failure of leadership may be reduced to the wide gap between popular expectations of what a president should do and the realities of what a president can do. It would be incorrect to claim that the presidency is no longer a powerful office. Nevertheless, there are greater constraints on any president's ability to exercise national leadership.

A president once could expect a degree of loyalty simply because he was the leader of a party. Now presidents may be elected as Democrats or Republicans, but they serve a nation that increasingly considers political parties irrelevant. Government has taken over most of the social services that used to be provided by the parties. (Whatever else one may say about political machines and machine politicians, they often provided citizens with a broad range of tangible benefits, asking nothing in return but their votes.) Television enables candidates to make themselves known directly to the voters without the aid of party apparatus. A society in which political parties have little impact denies the chief executive this base of support.

Some blame the presidency's problems on divided government. Since the end of World War II there have been twenty-three years in which the White House was controlled by one party and both chambers of Congress by the other. But the experiences of Democrats Carter and Clinton when serving with Democratic Congresses should make it evident that presidents can no longer expect much comfort from members of Congress merely because they share the same party label. What is true of a president is equally true of senators and representatives: their election is the result of their own efforts to achieve a personal following, not the efforts of a party machine. Rarely do they owe the president anything by virtue of his being head of the party. Furthermore, because it seems almost inevitable that a president is going to lose popularity as his time in office lengthens, it is to the interest of legislators belonging to the same party to dissociate themselves from him (and, of course, to attack him if they are of the opposition party).

Thus an American president is on his own. This puts tremendous demands on his ability to persuade. Presidents, of course, have virtually unlimited access to the means of communication. It is inconceivable that a president should give a speech or call a news conference and that no cameras and reporters would show up. Yet despite this access, all presidents face a common problem that was once described by Franklin Roosevelt in this way: "Individual psychology cannot be attuned for long periods of time to a constant repetition of the highest note in the scale." The paradox is that while modern presidents must often seek support directly from the people, the more they appeal directly, the less effective their appeals are apt to be. There is no way to repeal the law of diminishing returns. There are limits to how much public persuasion even the most artful speaker can accomplish before he loses his audience.

At the same time, presidents are having greater difficulties succeeding in private persuasion, such as bargaining for the support of legislators. One reason is that presidents have fewer rewards to offer than they once had. Out of a federal civilian workforce of more than 2 million, only about 3,000 are presidential appointees. Federal contracts are supposed to be awarded on the basis of competitive bidding. So the famous adage of nineteenth-century American politics, "To the victor belongs the spoils," no longer means much on the federal level; indeed some state governors have more patronage to distribute than does the president. Instead of divvying out economic rewards (jobs and contracts), presidents have been forced to apportion invitations to White House dinners and other symbolic rewards. However much coveted, symbolic rewards simply do not have the clout to swing a legislator into line that a job or a contract for a constituent would have.

Other constraints on the modern presidency result from the size and complexity of the federal government. Obviously it was a lot easier for a president to govern when he could gather in one room all of the people to whom he had delegated responsibilities. In our own age of big government, many federal executives must act in the name of the president without ever talking with him—even, in some cases, without ever having met him. Yet it is not just that government has become so much bigger, more bureaucratic, and less responsive. It is now expected to perform many tasks it was not formerly concerned with at all. These involve challenges such as cleaning up environmental pollution that would be incredibly difficult to meet under any circumstances. In an increasing number of instances, the government has either assumed or inherited technical, social, and economic problems that *nobody* has been able to cope with. Do educators really know why some children cannot read? Do economists really know how to deal with unemployment and inflation at the same time? Can anyone make an intelligent cost-benefit analysis of any new welfare program? Yet we turn for answers to the government, and specifically to the chief executive.

These are forces that work against all presidents. And, of course, unique or particular forces may affect any particular president. Franklin Roosevelt was in office on December 7, 1941, when Pearl Harbor was attacked; Carter was president when OPEC raised the price of oil in June 1979. In a typical week in April 1984 Reagan had to consider a successful coup in Guinea and a failed coup in Cameroon; fighting between Catholics and Protestants in Northern Ireland, Sikhs and Hindus in India, Moslems and Christians in Lebanon; terrorist attacks in Israel, South Africa, and Greece; and a war between Iran and Iraq. Presidents are increasingly buffeted by events beyond their control. They are held most closely responsible for the state of the domestic economy and for the state of international relations— the two areas in which there are the largest number of forces unresponsive to whatever controls a president might try to exercise.

As times change, so too do the exigencies of effective leadership. Eisenhower, for example, felt that his mission was to establish a sense of calm after what he viewed as the divisiveness engendered by Truman. Ford sought to make his mark through a candid and open mode of conduct after the behind-closed-doors presidency of Nixon. Carter, like Ford, had to preside over a country racked in a single decade by the Vietnam War and by Watergate. In practical terms, presidents now have to contend with a variety of congressional enactments designed to prevent future Vietnams and Watergates by placing constraints on their autonomy.

The American constitutional system of checks and balances often produces seesaw movements of president and Congress: when the president is up, Congress is down; when Congress is up, the presidency is down. Although there are advantages and disadvantages to the ascendancy of either, the teeter-totter principle is for better or worse the way American government seeks a golden mean. The difficulty is how to reach the mean, how to put together an effective collaborative leadership combining the best that a specific Congress and president have to offer. It has happened from time to time in our history, but not often.

In the wake of twin national disasters, Vietnam and Watergate, Congress assumed an assertive attitude. This was especially evident in foreign affairs, the realm in which presidents traditionally had the greatest leeway to act in the name of the nation. Whether in treaty making, or the stance taken on specific disputes, or broad-gauge policy matters, Congress made it clear that it no longer intended to be a president's rubber stamp. In some instances the members were merely responding to constituent groups—Americans of Polish or Irish descent, for example—just as they respond to constituents on domestic issues. But congressional involvement in foreign affairs also reflected the emergence of a new-style legislator: younger, better educated, with more interest in issues beyond the borders of his or her own district.

Vietnam and Watergate, of course, profoundly affected the American people as well as their representatives in Washington. These events, and such persistent problems as crime, inflation, and unemployment shook confidence in those who run governments—legislators, executives, jurists—and at all levels. The problem has not been one of the presidency alone.

This attitude is partly fed by the news media, which, by definition in a free society, look for and report on all malefactions of the public trust. Things that are right about the government are sometimes news, though not often; but all the things that are wrong are sure to be reported if they can be uncovered. Presidents since Washington have had their problems with the press, but leaders now must learn to live with much closer scrutiny. In an earlier age, trust in the president was the norm. A president had to earn popular distrust by some specific iniquity such as the Teapot Dome scandal of Warren Harding's administration. Now the reverse may be true. "As Americans are becoming more informed politically," Paul Peterson has commented, "they are rightly critical of institutions and practices that they once accepted on faith."

A frequently suggested reform for what ails the presidency is a constitutional amendment creating a single, six-year term. The main idea is that, since the president would not have to be running for a second term throughout his first, he could risk being bold, innovative, and resourceful. At least, the risk need not involve political suicide. Former Senator Mike Mansfield stated the rationale thus:

> A President under a single, six-year term would not be removed entirely from politics, but the amount of time he would have to allot to politics would be decreased considerably, and by the same token the amount of time he would be able to spend on looking after the national interest, both domestically and in the field of foreign policy, would be increased.

The notion of "depoliticizing" the presidency, whatever its virtues, is not universally applauded. What we are dealing with, Thomas E. Cronin has said,

> is a highly political office and it cannot be otherwise; its political character is for the most part desirable. Efforts to remove it from politics are naive and politically harmful. An apolitical presidency, uninterested in re-election, and aloof from concerns of the great political parties, would probably be a highly irresponsible presidency.

On a less theoretical level, the problem with the proposal is that if a good president were elected, the nation would have him in the

White House for two years less than under the present system, and if a bad president were elected, the American people would be stuck with the consequences for two years longer than under the present system.

In addition to schemes for changing the rules regarding the president's term of office, a great deal of attention has been devoted to potential means of freeing the chief executive from what Henry Steele Commager calls "the endless demands on his time and thought, endless demands . . . which distract him from the main task of leadership." Ideas for improving this situation include a suggestion from Milton Eisenhower to create two executive vice presidents— one to supervise domestic agencies, the other for international relations—with the president relieved of day-to-day management responsibilities. A former U.S. representative, Henry S. Reuss of Wisconsin, thinks that in addition to the president there should be "an elected Chief of State [who] would free the President from many of the draining ceremonial functions which now occupy much of his time." Such schemes, of course, are based on the premise that the job has become too much for one person to handle. But many scholars doubt that the constitutional duties of the presidency are divisible without causing friction and stalemate; there can be only one leader of the executive branch at a time.

Those who would tinker with the form of the presidency—or would move toward a parliamentary mode of governing—may be overlooking the considerable capacity for self-correction that was built into the present system. Some of the factors that work to the disadvantage of the president are reversible. If Congress is up today, the whole of American history suggests that there will come a time when the seesaw tilts back and the president will be up again. This happens when Congress stumbles badly, as badly as presidents did during Vietnam and Watergate. A most likely congressional stumbling block is foreign affairs, where there is little evidence to indicate that a 535-member legislature is in a better position to make effective policy than the president is. Also, almost surely there will come a time—probably during a sustained period of economic growth— when the American people will have a far more sanguine attitude about political leaders in general, and presidents will be allowed more latitude to act.

By recounting the new realities that make it more difficult to do a good job of being president, I do not mean to imply that it makes no difference who is in the White House, or that the burdens are now such as to sink any occupant. George Washington, Andrew Jackson, and Abraham Lincoln were not great presidents simply because they lived in earlier times. There are obvious qualities of wisdom, imagination, even daring that distinguish one president from another and that have not died out in contemporary civilization. There are skills of language, judgment, and negotiation that leaders either learn or seem to be born with. Then, too, some people are just plain lucky, which is a desirable quality for presidents to have. And we are finding out a great deal about personality type vis-à-vis the presidential office. Some people are more fit psychologically to be president than others and can make a special creative endeavor out of exercising power in a democratic framework. A fortunate advantage of the American system is that the Constitution places very few restrictions on who can be president. The parliamentary system requires that the prime minister come from the legislature, but Americans can cast their net almost as wide as they can imagine. Any native-born citizen over the age of thirty-five is eligible.

Presidents *are* restricted in their actions, and that is by fundamental design. James Madison commented that the founders of the American republic were primarily worried about "the overgrown and all-grasping prerogative of an hereditary magistrate." So the basic question, then and always, is how much power the people should entrust to a leader. The powers of the president are considerable, even if the constraints are also considerable. The powers and constraints, however, are fluid. They change in reaction to past events and in relation to present circumstances. They change, too, as presidents display different degrees of wisdom, skill, and fortitude in leading the nation.

# Index